Rights

Responsibilities

and the Law

Thomas Nelson and Sons Ltd
Nelson House   Mayfield Road
Walton-on-Thames   Surrey
KT12 5PL   UK

51 York Place
Edinburgh
EH1 3JD   UK

Thomas Nelson (Hong Kong) Ltd
Toppan Building 10/F
22A Westlands Road
Quarry Bay   Hong Kong

Thomas Nelson (Kenya) Ltd
P.O. Box 18123
Nairobi   Kenya

Distributed in Australia by

Thomas Nelson Australia
480 La Trobe Street
Melbourne   Victoria 3000
and in Sydney, Brisbane, Adelaide and Perth

© Thomas Nelson and Sons Ltd/ILEA Learning Materials Service/Cobden Trust 1982
First published by Thomas Nelson and Sons Ltd in association with
ILEA Learning Materials Service and the Cobden Trust 1982
Reprinted 1983 (twice), 1984, 1986, 1987
ISBN 0-17-438190-5
NPN 04

Printed and bound in Hong Kong

Contents

Introduction

One of the causes of injustice is ignorance. The young person who spends months in prison awaiting trial may not realise that he or she can apply for bail. Many of the people who each year appear in Magistrates' Courts unrepresented by a solicitor do not know that they are entitled to legal aid. Young people often don't know how to begin finding their way through the complex laws which govern their lives.

The Cobden Trust was established in 1963 to carry out research into causes of injustice and to help people learn about civil liberties in practice. Its work on civil liberties in the United Kingdom grew directly out of the experience of the National Council for Civil Liberties, whose casework revealed that human rights problems were not confined to other countries.

Rights, Responsibilities and the Law is designed to meet a gap in the materials used in schools. It has three aims: to help people to acquire practical *information* about this country's laws, how they are made, and what each citizen's rights and duties are; to encourage *debate* about controversial issues which affect all of us in our day-to-day lives; and to develop the *skills* which allow people to find their way round the system as they grow up.

Because the emphasis is on information and ideas which will be of practical use, this is not a sociology textbook, a history textbook, or a book aimed at any other particular discipline. The teachers and students who tested this material found it useful in a very wide range of humanities courses — general studies, English, history, social studies and so on.

A large part of this book grew out of requests from teachers and students. Some of it may be controversial, but it is not propaganda! On issues where there is considerable disagreement, a number of points of view are given, and throughout the book as much information as possible about what the law says and how it works is provided, so that the issues can be fully discussed.

Finally, the Cobden Trust would like to thank all the people who put so much hard work into this project. The Gulbenkian Foundation provided an extremely generous grant which allowed us to employ an education officer for three years to research, write and trial the book; their director, Peter Brinson, gave us invaluable and enthusiastic support. The final year's work on the project was most generously assisted by the Gatsby Foundation. The staff of the Learning Materials Service of the Inner London Education Authority — particularly Peter Weiss, Andy Hudson, Prue Chennells and Cathy Moorhouse — were a pleasure to work with, and ensured that the needs of students and teachers received priority throughout. Our publishers, Thomas Nelson and Sons Ltd, ensured that the first draft of this book was tested in schools all over the country and their editors, Pam Bowen and Sharon Behr, worked closely with the production team throughout. We were greatly assisted by a group of teachers who helped to formulate ideas for the book, and went on helping by correcting drafts and using them in their classrooms; among them we must single out Bob Dade of Broxbourne School, who approached us before we even got the project off the ground. We would also like to thank Inspector C.M. Leithead of the Metropolitan Police Community Relations Branch for his generous contribution of time and effort. A number of NCCL lawyers have helped us to ensure that the book is as accurate as possible, and we would particularly like to thank Peter Thornton, NCCL's chairperson, for his active involvement. Finally we want to thank our two education officers, Cath Prior and Judith Edmunds, without whom this book would never have been produced.

Patricia Hewitt
Trustee, Cobden Trust

Most of the cases cited in the text are based on real incidents; in some cases, however, names have been fictionalised to provide anonymity for the individuals or organisations involved.

Chapter One

Why laws?

Stranded!

A group of sixteen-year-olds is on a school cruise in the Pacific Ocean. A sudden storm wrecks the ship. The students manage to climb into a small lifeboat, and are eventually washed ashore on a desert island.

Now read on . . .

Steve jumped off the boat.
'Right! You girls get looking for food, and we'll build some shelters.'
Steve was the biggest boy in the group and was used to getting his own way, but even so there were a lot of angry murmurs.
Mary spoke up.
'Says who? Nobody tells me what to do. I'm going to look after myself, that's all.'

'You wouldn't say that for long if you were ill,' said Graham. 'You'd want someone else to look after you then, wouldn't you?'
'What if I found the only food on the island?' Jane added. 'You'd want me to share it round, wouldn't you, and not keep it all for myself? I don't want Steve to boss us all about either, but I do think we should share things.'

'I think the most important thing is to find a way off the island,' said Anne. Jane disagreed.
'No, the most important thing is to find food,' she replied.
'See!' shouted Steve. 'Everybody is arguing already. We need someone in charge to tell the others what to do. We need some rules. We'll all be fighting in a minute.'
'I can do without your rules,' said Anne. 'You'd have all of us running round after you while you sat giving orders.'
Graham nodded in agreement.
'Maybe we do need some rules,' he said. 'But I don't see that one person has to make them. Surely we should all agree on what we need to do, then we can all make sure that things get done.'
Steve moved towards Graham. He towered over him.
'Oh yeah? he said, threateningly.

What would you do?

In the story, Steve thinks that as he is the strongest member of the group, the others should do as he wants. Graham thinks that everyone should agree about the decisions to be made. Mary thinks that things would be all right if people just looked after themselves.

First write down everything you can think of to support (a) Steve's point of view, (b) Graham's point of view, (c) Mary's point of view. You might like to do this in groups.

Then imagine that it's your group stranded on that desert island. You have some important decisions to make, and you will need to overcome certain problems if your community is to survive. For example, how would you get **food and water?**

Do you think that a small group should look for food and water and share it out according to who needs most?

Or that the people who do the most work should get the most food?

Or that everybody should take it in turns to find food because everybody eats, and the food should be shared out equally?

Discuss these suggestions with your group, and decide which rules to adopt.

Now think about how your group would deal with (a) property, (b) settling disputes and (c) caring for the sick. Again, there will be differences of opinion, and you will have to agree on rules to adopt.

Finally, prepare a magazine feature based on the experience of being stranded.

1 Describe the shipwreck.

2 Describe the island and draw a detailed map.

3 Describe the ways in which your group was able to survive: how they solved the problems of food, water, shelter, clothing and so on.

Rules, responsibilities and rights

On the desert island, the group found that they needed some kinds of rules to share things out, to settle disputes, to care for the sick, and to solve many other problems that arise when people live together. Making those rules entails giving people **rights** as well as giving them **responsibilities**.

If you want the right to keep what is yours, then you have the responsibility to respect what is someone else's, and to ensure that others do the same.

If you want the right to be cared for when you are ill, then you have the responsibility to care for others — or to ensure that they receive care — when they are ill.

Sometimes your rights are affected because of your responsibilities: you have the right to freedom of speech, but you have to use that right in a responsible way. This means you shouldn't use it to incite others to racial hatred, for example.

Keeping a balance between the rights of the individual and the good of the majority can create problems. In most communities, an organised system of laws is developed to protect people's rights and to enforce their responsibilities.

In Britain, the system of law is very complicated. This is because it has developed over hundreds of years. It is difficult to compile a list of the individual's rights at any one time.

British laws are made by Parliament, but the way they are operated is left to the courts. Individual judges reach decisions in individual cases, and these decisions create **precedents** for later cases. So if you had to appear in court, the people representing you — solicitors and barristers — would look back through previous cases to see if a case involving similar principles had established a precedent. If so, this precedent would probably be followed in deciding a verdict in your case. British law is therefore based on 'creating a binding precedent'.

Young people and the law

People under the age of eighteen usually find that their rights are more restricted by the law than those of adults. Most of the laws that affect young people are protective, because Parliament believes that they still need protection and cannot be held totally responsible for all their actions.

Young people sometimes complain that they're regarded as too young to do the things they want to do. But being a juvenile (under seventeen) also brings certain advantages: for example, if you're under seventeen you can't, as a general rule, be sent to prison.

The list in the box shows you the ages at which you gain certain rights by law.

Richard and Sally Greenhill

Tony Othen

Homer Sykes

From birth

You can have an account in your name with a bank or a building society

You can have premium bonds in your name

You can have a passport of your own (if one of your parents signs the application form)

At age 5

You can drink alcohol legally in private

At age 7

You can see an A certificate film without an adult

You can draw money from a post office or savings account

At age 10

You can be convicted of a criminal offence if it is proved that you knew the difference between right and wrong

At age 12

You can buy a pet animal

At age 13

You can be employed for a certain number of hours a week (see page 102)

At age 14

You can be held fully responsible for a crime

You can be fingerprinted if you are in custody and charged

You can be convicted of a sexual offence (applies to boys only)

You can see an AA certificate film

You can pawn an article in a pawn shop

You can go into a pub, but not drink or buy alcohol there

At age 15

You can be sent to Borstal

You can be sent to prison to await trial (applies to boys only)

At age 16

You can buy premium bonds

You can sell scrap metal

You can buy cigarettes or tobacco

You can join a trade union

You can leave school

You can choose your own doctor

You can claim social security benefit

You can work full-time

You can have sexual intercourse (applies to girls only: if a girl under sixteen has sexual intercourse, her partner, the boy, is liable to prosecution)

You can leave home with your parents' consent

You can get married with one parent's consent

You can drink wine or beer with a meal in a restaurant

You can buy fireworks

You can hold a licence to drive a moped, motor cycle, certain tractors or invalid carriages

At age 17

You can hold a licence to drive any vehicle except certain heavy ones

You can be sent to prison

You can appear before adult courts

You can engage in street trading

At age 18

You can leave home without your parents' consent

You can get married without your parents' consent

You can vote

You can act as executor of a person's will

You can make a will

You can see an X certificate film

You can bet

You can change your name

You can apply for a passport

You can buy and sell goods

You can own houses and land

You can buy on hire purchase

You can apply for a mortgage

You can sue and be sued

You can go abroad to sing, play or perform professionally

You can sit on a jury

You can be a blood donor

You can buy alcohol

You can drink alcohol in a pub

At age 21

You can stand in a Parliamentary or local election

You can drive any mechanically propelled vehicle

You can hold a licence to sell alcohol

You can take part in a homosexual relationship (applies to boys only: see page 77)

You can adopt a child

1 Make a list of all the rules your school has. Find out:
● whether they are all written down in one place
● how people coming to school learn what the rules are
● whether there is a definite punishment for breaking each of the rules

2 Divide your list of rules into those you think are:
● worth having
● not worth having

Either write down, or discuss, your reasons for thinking the rules are important or unimportant.

3 Who do you think should make the school rules? Why?

4 Would it be possible to run a school without any rules at all?

5 If you need some school rules, make a list of what they should be. Say how you would make sure they were obeyed.

6 If you have the right to be looked after when you are old, then you have a responsibility to look after the old. Think of six rights and put them in a sentence like this one, along with the corresponding responsibility.

Whose right?

In each of the following stories, one person's rights are effectively limiting those of another person. In each case, there are problems . . .

Pete's party

Pete would soon be fifteen. He wanted to celebrate with his friends and thought of throwing a party. He talked to his parents about this. 'But Annie and Pauline *always* come round here on a Saturday night,' protested his mother. 'It's the only time we get a chance to sit down and talk.'

'And what about the carpet?' his father asked. 'Five hundred quid's worth of good pile there — what happens if one of your friends spills his food all over it?'
'Oh, don't worry,' replied Pete. 'I'll make sure all the food stays in the kitchen. And Mum, you and your friends meet every week — I only have a birthday once a year.'
Pete's parents reluctantly agreed to the party.

Before the weekend, one of Pete's friends, John, brought his sound system around to Pete's house. 'Boy, we'll blow their ears off with this,' he told Pete. 'Let's make sure we borrow some LPs from the kids at school.'

The night of the party, Pete cleared his parents' front room. The sofa was pushed against the wall and the television and ornaments moved to a safe place. Pete's parents went out to the cinema, and Pete's friend Jill came round to help him prepare the food. They bought drinks and set up the sound system.

By 10 o'clock the party was in full swing. People were dancing in the front room, others were eating in the kitchen and some were sitting talking on the stairs.
Suddenly there was a banging on the door. Pete went to answer it. On the doorstep he found two police officers.
'Well,' said one of them, 'having a party?'
'Yes,' replied Pete, a bit worried.
'Well, it's too noisy. Your neighbours have complained. One of them has two young children and they can't get a wink of sleep. And what about that old lady next door — eighty-six if she's a day, and she's not so keen on reggae.'
As Pete shut the door, and went to turn the music down, one of his friends was sick all over Pete's parents' carpet.
'Oh, no,' thought Pete, 'what else can go wrong?'

Barbara and babysitting

Barbara was fed up. She was babysitting for her baby sister, and it was Saturday night.

Barbara's parents went out every Saturday night, and she was left holding the baby! As they said, it was the only night they managed to go out together. But Barbara was sixteen — she sometimes wanted to go out on a Saturday night, too. She hated having to stay in, listening to the noise that came from the baby's bedroom every so often. She felt helpless.

Joe loses his job

Only one more term to go! Joe could hardly wait. The teacher's voice droned on in the distance as Joe sat dreaming of the job waiting for him in the printing works. He thought about how good it was going to be to get his first wages and how lucky he was to have a job to go to.

His daydream was interrupted by the sound of the school bell. Joe grabbed his bag and rushed for the gate. He rounded the corner into the high street, where he caught sight of a news-stand hoarding. He blinked, hoping he had dreamt it, but when he opened his eyes again he read the poster out loud: 'Teachers' union says raise school leaving age.' Joe just couldn't believe what he was reading — how could they? And now of all times, just as he was about to launch himself on a whole new future. He'd lose the job; they'd not want to wait a year before they took him on. Joe's anguish turned to rage. All those bottled-up feelings began to rise inside and he turned automatically and started back towards the school. Before he knew it, he was in the school entrance hall, and standing there was Mr Green,

the deputy head.
'You ... it's all your silly fault ...' said Joe, and he flung himself across the entrance hall, his fists clenched ...
A sudden crunching thud brought Joe to his senses, and he was pinned to the floor, unable to move. Out of the corner of his eye he saw the face of his friend, Billy Wallace.
'What are you up to, you idiot?' said Billy, tightening his hold on Joe.
'Do you want to wind up inside?'

1 Joe was all set to make a big scene about raising the school leaving age. Do you think he went about this in the right way? Discuss this with your group.

2 Certain rights were being limited by Pete's party: those of his parents, and those of his neighbours. Discuss what those rights were.

3 In Barbara's case, whose rights were being limited? As a group, can you agree on a compromise?

4 Write a story or play in which Barbara explains her feelings, listens to her parents' point of view, and tries to reach a compromise.

5 Sarah was shopping in a store in the high street. She was at the counter when she saw a woman putting a sweater into her shopping bag. Discuss what you would have done if you had been in Sarah's position. Would you have:
● reported the incident to the staff?
● gone up to the woman and told her to put it back?
● thought if she could get away with it, good luck to her?
● decided you didn't really want to get involved? How would you justify your choice?

6 How far do you think people should go to show their opposition to something? Are people ever justified in breaking the law? Write your views.

Changing the law

In the story about Joe, he felt that the law was unfair and that it should be changed. Here is an example of how people can help to change laws.

1833

The story begins in 1833. Women in the Glasgow Spinners' Association met to demand the same pay as men, for doing the same work. It was the first recorded claim of this kind.

1900

One group of women (the suffragettes) were prepared to break the law in order to get what they believed was their right — the vote. Other women, too, campaigned, marched and petitioned to get public sympathy for their cause.

1914

Mansell Collection

During the First World War, women took over many of the jobs done by men, and politicians realised that they could no longer claim that there were certain jobs that women could not do.

1928

Women finally got the vote in 1928, but getting the vote did not bring equality, or equal pay.

1930s

In the 1930s women began to put pressure on the trade unions to fight for equal pay.

16

What do people do to campaign?

Here are some of the things people did in the campaign for equal pay:
● persuaded the trade unions to support women in their places of work, or nationally
● demonstrated, picketed, or went on strike if equal pay was refused

● asked other trade unions and sympathetic groups, like women's organisations, to support them
● went to people in the public eye, like MPs, TV personalities and local councillors for support

● demonstrated in the street, or held meetings in- and out-of-doors
● collected evidence to show that the law needed changing, and presented it in leaflets, or letters to newspapers, to tell people about it

1950s

By the 1950s, women teachers, civil servants and some other professional workers had achieved equal pay, but most other women still received under 60 per cent of a man's wage, even when they did exactly the same work.

1960s

In 1963, the TUC passed a resolution calling for quick legislation on equal pay. Many women's organisations began lobbying MPs, and getting support in the Press for better child welfare benefits, more nurseries, changes in the tax laws, equal educational opportunities and equal job opportunities.

During the late 1960s, there were several strikes because women were refused equal pay. One of the biggest was at Ford (Dagenham) in 1968. All these events led to questions and discussion in Parliament.

In 1970, the Equal Pay Act was passed. It said that women and men were to be paid the same for the same kind of work. It finally came into force in 1975 — nearly 150 years after the struggle began.

---

1 Find one example of each of the following: a pressure group; a demonstration; a petition; a letter to the papers; a leaflet. Write about one of these examples.

2 Think of a law or rule that you would like to see changed, or a local issue that worries you. How would you set about campaigning?

3 Some people say that it's all right for factory workers to strike, but not for nurses. What reasons might they give for this view? Do you think everyone should have an equal right to strike?

4 If there is a local campaign group in your area, with the headteacher's permission ask a representative of the group to visit the school to tell you how they are going about their campaign. Collect leaflets, newspaper cuttings and other details for a display, and write about their campaign.

How a law is made

For many years people campaigned to get Parliament to recognise the need for women to have equal pay in Britain. This is how the Equal Pay Act came into being.

1. Dissatisfaction

GROUP PRESSURE

But I do exactly the same job as you do!

£67·50

£90

THE PRESS

DAILY POST

PARTY IN FAVOUR OF CHANGE ON EQUAL PAY

But bosses ask: equal pay for the same or similar work? And how will they decide who gets paid wh...

Delegates, I ask you to vote to back the motion that the Party supports the introduction of equal pay legislation at the earliest possible opportunity.

PARTY CONFERENCE

2. The Green Paper

After a great deal of pressure, the Labour Government produced a Green Paper. This document raises points for public discussion.

3. The White Paper

A White Paper is a list of aims that the Government wants to make into laws.

4. A Bill is drafted

CONTINUED

5. House of Commons debate

FIRST READING

The Bill is drafted a number of times in the Commons. The first reading is really just an announcement that the Bill is coming.

SECOND READING

The second reading is a more lengthy debate. Then a vote is taken on whether the Bill should go forward.

Equal pay in itself is not good enough. Britain needs a law to ensure equal opportunity.

How is equal pay defined – 'equal pay for the same work' is far too easy to avoid: employers will simply make sure that women and men do different jobs.

The expense of giving equal pay is going to slow down economic recovery in Britain.

STANDING COMMITTEE

19 February to 7 March
The points raised in the House of Commons debate are discussed. MPs have pointed out many weaknesses in the Bill, and these have to be improved by a committee who discuss and redraft the Bill.

Interested organisations outside the House of Commons also examine the Bill, and let their MPs know if they think there is something that should be changed ...

COMMITTEE REPORT AND THIRD READING

22 and 23 April
... then the Bill is reintroduced and discussed further ...

The same or broadly similar work ...

The new wording is obviously better but it is going to take some time for workers and management to get together and work out rates for women doing work that is 'broadly similar.'

6. House of Lords debate

This Act might produce a situation of greater discrimination against women if it is not carefully worded. Employers may cut back and women lose their jobs as a result.

Bills may be debated again, going back and forth between the House of Commons and the House of Lords until agreement is reached. But the Equal Pay Act went straight from the Lords to the final committee stages for detailed changes.

7. Royal assent

The Queen signed the Equal Pay Bill on 29 May 1970, and so the provisions of the Act became law.

8. Act put into practice

EQUAL PAY ACT PASSED

In this particular case, Parliament and the various committees had decided that the law should not come into force immediately, but that time should be allowed for employers and unions to work out the implications. The law would operate from 29 December 1975. From that date, employers ignoring the Act could be taken to court.

Of course, the way the judges interpret the law affects the way the law operates in practice.

The above information is simplified and it is important to realise that:
• laws rarely pass through all the stages as smoothly as this
• many things that people feel passionately about don't get taken up by Parliament at all

What would you do?

1 In Britain, we have equal pay for the same work or work that is 'broadly similar'. How would you decide if the following two people should be paid the same amount?

Ms Graham works as a chef cooking lunch each day for six directors of a large factory, and for their guests. Mr Dancy works in the factory canteen in charge of preparing lunch for 300 employees each day. Ms Graham earns £95 per week, Mr Dancy earns £120 per week. Ms Graham claims that she should be paid the same amount as Mr Dancy.

The questions you will need to ask and answer should cover every aspect of the two jobs. For example:
• how the two employees spend their working hours
• the number of people each caters for
• the responsibilities each has
Try to imagine yourself doing each job; this will help you to work out what further questions you need to ask.

2 You have read about the various stages that any proposed new legislation has to pass through before it finally becomes law. Now divide into groups and decide upon a new law you would like to see passed if you were MPs. Then work out and write down exactly what you would want it to say. You might like to present the draft of your proposed new law to the other groups and ask for criticisms and suggestions for improvement of the wording. Afterwards, you could return to your own group to finalise exactly what your new law will say.

Once you have decided upon the law you want to create, you will need to consider:
• to whom it should apply — and who, if anyone, should be exempted from it
• how to word it so that it is clear and not confusing
• how it can be enforced — for example, what can be done to encourage people to obey it, and what sanctions will be brought against people who disobey it

A law in practice

I'm the Gentlemen's Edulcorator and I earn £45

I'm the Ladies' Lav cleaner and I earn £30

Vive la différence!

GENTS   LADIES

The Equal Pay Act 1970

The Equal Pay Act says a woman should have equal pay if:
● she is doing the same or similar work as a man
● her job has been given the same value as a man's job under a job evaluation scheme (Professional people are employed to study jobs and grade how much they are worth. Jobs with the same grade should have the same money.)

Under the Act, individuals who feel they are being unfairly treated can take cases to **industrial tribunals**. These are made up of a chairperson (who is a lawyer), a person put forward by a trade union, and another put forward by an employers' organisation. If the decision reached by the tribunal doesn't satisfy the individual, he or she may appeal to an **employment appeal tribunal**. The chairperson of this tribunal is a judge. A case can go through the Court of Appeal to the House of Lords.

Does the Act apply to men?

Yes. If men are not treated as well as women who are doing the same work, then they can claim equal pay and conditions, too. For example, men in the police force successfully claimed a special shoe allowance which had previously only been given to women.

Has The Equal Pay Act given women equal rights?

The Equal Pay Act 1970	October 1976 - September 1977	October 1977- September 1978
Total number of applications	942	454
Number of cases settled without a tribunal	57	33
Number of cases withdrawn	393	234
Number of cases won at tribunal	175	42
Number of cases dismissed at tribunal	317	145

Work and play

A female community worker believed she should be paid on the same scale as the man working with her as a playleader. They both agreed that most of their work overlapped. The only differences between the two were that the female had overall responsibility for the project where they worked — and she got about £400 a year and two weeks' holiday less than her male colleague.

The industrial tribunal which heard the case, in April 1976, said that the greater responsibility held by the female was of such importance that equal pay could not be justified. They believed she should be paid more than the male playleader, but they were not empowered to award more. An appeal to an Employment Appeal Tribunal ordered that the case be reheard, since the wrong approach had been taken to the law, but another tribunal still ruled against her.

Cutting corners

A woman who cut curtains wanted the same pay as a man who cut blinds. The tribunal said, 'Blind cutting is mostly done by a knife along a straight edge of the cutting table. Curtain cutting normally involves marking the fabric first and then cutting the marked fabric with scissors or shears.' The man's job was considered a 'heavier and generally bigger operation'. The tribunal also said, 'It may be that if there was a proper job evaluation, the female's job would be given a greater value than that of the male blind cutter.'

Light or heavy workers

A representative of 70 women who worked as paint-can fillers at a factory got in touch with the National Council for Civil Liberties. The firm was trying to prevent an equal pay claim by calling the women 'light paint-can fillers' and putting them on a lower grade than the men. The men did identical work alongside the women, but were now called 'heavy paint-can fillers'. The NCCL looked into the case, and told the union representative at the factory that they would probably win their case in law. He went to the management and arranged a successful equal pay deal within 24 hours.

So, passing a law doesn't mean an instant change in conditions.

British law is based on precedent, and the way the law works in practice depends on the cases that have been brought, and on the decisions made for those cases.

Most women don't work alongside men, but in separate jobs where there are few or no men with whom they can be compared.

The Act is very complicated and many employers have found ways to avoid paying women the same wages as men, for example:
● by cutting down on the number of jobs done by both men **and** women
● by giving jobs different names so that men and women aren't doing 'the same job'
● by promoting men to higher positions

1 Do you think there is any reason why a man and a woman doing identical jobs should not get equal pay?

2 Should there be some jobs for men only, and others for women only? If so, which ones, and why?

3 Why don't women on the whole get equal pay?

4 What percentage of cases were won in tribunal courts under The Equal Pay Act 1970 between
(a) October 1976 and September 1977
(b) October 1977 and September 1978?

5 Would you like to do a job that was done mainly by the opposite sex? (For example boys: would you like to be a secretary? girls: would you like to be an electrician?) What would be the advantages and disadvantages of being in such a minority?

6 Make a list of the jobs done by all the men you know personally. Make a similar list for the women you know. Compare the lists, and comment on similarities and differences.

7 Count how many hours each person in your family spends at work. Take 'work' to mean paid employment in or out of the home, housework and work at school. Compare the kinds of work each of you does. Who does most, and why?

Private Members' Bills

On pages 18 to 21 you read about how a law is made: the Government (the party in power) produces a Green Paper and then a White Paper, the Bill is debated several times in the House of Commons and then in the House of Lords and, finally, after general agreement and much detailed work, it becomes law.

“There is another way for Parliament to make laws, or change existing ones. This is by **Private Members' Bills** — Bills introduced by individual Members of Parliament. But because most Parliamentary time is taken up with carrying out Government policy, there are only ten days available each year for back-bench MPs to have their say. (Back-benchers are MPs of any party who are not Cabinet Members.) There is a ballot every year for a chance to introduce a Bill. Up to twenty Members' names are drawn and the nearer they are to the top of the ballot, the greater the chance of the Bill being debated and becoming law.

In practice, only about six Private Members' Bills get through.

If the proposals in a Bill are controversial, or if they involve spending large amounts of public money, the Government will oppose them. So the subjects chosen are usually about matters on which the Government hasn't stated a political view — subjects which they are content to leave to Parliament as a whole to decide upon. One example was the 1967 Abortion Act, which gives women limited rights to obtain abortion. It was introduced as a Private Members' Bill by David Steel, Liberal MP for Argyll and Bute.”

Jo Richardson MP, who successfully introduced a Private Member's Bill designed to protect women from violence by their partners: the Domestic Violence Act 1976.

Press Association

Chapter Two

Policing

Policing through the ages

We cannot imagine being without the police force — we've come to look on it as a fact of life. But until 150 years ago it didn't exist. So how was law maintained before that, and who made sure that people kept order?

A typical 17th century 'Charlie'

Mary Evans

Anglo-Saxon times

In Anglo-Saxon times, village people divided up into groups of ten. If any member of the group committed a crime, the others were responsible for bringing him or her to trial, and could be punished themselves for not doing so. Anyone who saw a crime taking place had to raise the alarm (then called 'raising a hue and cry'), and villagers stopped what they were doing to chase the criminal.

A hue and cry:
villagers chasing a thief

The Middle Ages

The Norman kings adopted many Anglo-Saxon law-keeping methods, but they also used their own sheriffs to strengthen control over the people and to make sure they kept an eye on each other. Constables were chosen by the manor court to help the lord of the manor, or baron, keep the peace. These constables were responsible for reporting villagers' behaviour, arresting criminals, and raising the hue and cry.

In 1361, Justices of the Peace were chosen, three reliable local people from each county, who were allowed to operate the law of the land.

The Tudors and Stuarts

The Tudor and Stuart kings wanted to reduce the power of the barons and of the Church, and they gave the Justices of the Peace and the constables more power to ensure that the king's laws were kept. These Justices and constables received no pay.

In 1663, the City of London paid a small group of old men to work as watchmen in the city at night. They were often too old and doddery to be any use and were called 'Charlies'.

For many years, the Justices of the Peace, the constables and the watchmen were responsible for keeping law and order in Britain.

Mary Evans

Conditions in 18th century London: disorder, poverty and drunkenness

Mary Evans

Panic in Manchester: the battle of Peterloo

Mansell Collection

A group of 'Peelers' 1851

The eighteenth century

During the eighteenth century, people began to move in great numbers out of the country into the new cities, and very soon the problems became too great for a few old watchmen to handle.

Squalid housing and sanitation together with high unemployment led to social unrest. Poverty, drunkenness, crime and rioting were almost out of hand, particularly in London. In 1748 Henry Fielding, a magistrate, organised a small force of regular, paid constables in London, based in Bow Street. This force was known as the 'Bow Street Runners'.

In 1780, Lord George Gordon, a politician with strong anti-Catholic views, stirred up a London mob. They marched on Parliament to protest at laws designed to make life easier for Catholics. This began six days of rioting. London was only saved when the army moved in: even so, 700 people were killed and great damage was done to buildings. Officials started talking about a paid force to keep order in the city.

The nineteenth century

Living conditions got worse in many parts of the country. Men who came back from the Napoleonic wars were unable to find work, and crime and violence on the streets increased. In 1819, large crowds assembled in Manchester for a political rally to protest against living conditions. The army panicked and opened fire on the crowd, and many people were killed. This angered the public and politicians alike.

In 1822, Robert Peel became Home Secretary and began to argue for a permanent police force. Seven years later, the Metropolitan Police Act was passed, giving London the first full police force in England. Constables were nicknamed 'Peelers' or 'Bobbies' after Robert Peel.

At first, people were afraid that the Government would use the police as a force of spies and bullies: poor people thought their terrible living conditions would

be made even worse, and many of the middle classes objected to a Government agency having the right to interfere in private disputes.

So the police force was attacked by criminals and ordinary citizens alike. The new Metropolitan Police Force worked only in London. It was not until 1856 that the Government made it compulsory for every county to have a police force, and inspectors were appointed to supervise them.

From the beginning, the police have worked hard to gain the acceptance and co-operation of the public. The range of work that they do has expanded enormously. The last hundred years has seen the development of the Criminal Investigation Department (CID), women police, motorised patrols and many other changes. You might like to do some research into how the police have changed.

?

1 Do you think it would be a good or a bad idea for individuals to form groups and be responsible for each other's behaviour today, as they did in Anglo-Saxon times? Give reasons for your answer.

2 Why do you think politicians and the public objected to the army being used to control demonstrations in the nineteenth century?

3 Can you think of any reasons why London was the first place to have a full, paid police force?

4 Do you think that people's attitudes to the police have changed since 1829? Give some reasons for your answers.

5 How do you think the police should, or will, change over the next twenty years? What sort of police force would you like to see?

6 Look at the table of police **maxims** (general principles) written in about 1840, on page 40.
a) How many of these things do you think are still relevant today?
b) What do they tell us about the image that the police have tried to create?
c) What other maxims would your group add for police in the 1980s? Write your own list.

A police officer's lot...

All police officers train for fifteen weeks at the police college at Hendon before going to their stations. Then they get on-the-job training and two days in the classroom each month. All officers work eight-hour shifts, arranged so that everybody does an equal number of different shifts.

This is how one police officer describes his work.

Sometimes calls over the radio are to the scene of a crime. This can be, rarely, to a murder. I'll never forget the time I was called to what I thought was my first murder. I went to a room where a woman was lying face-down with her head in a pool of blood. I was relieved to find out that she had not been murdered but had collapsed from a heart attack and bumped her nose when she fell.

More often these calls are to a minor theft or burglary, but however small the crime, it always has enormous consequences for the victim. The theft of £10 from an old age pensioner will cause much hardship, and even the loss of a small trinket can bring great personal sadness. People try to separate the law enforcement side from the social side of our work, but you can't. I remember going to a burglary where the thieves had piled all the contents of the drawers and cupboards in the middle of each room. I couldn't help thinking that if it had been my house, I wouldn't have known where to begin to tidy up.

" It's a frightening feeling when you first go out in uniform and realise people might actually come up and ask you something, even though you always go out with an experienced colleague at first. I'll never forget my first day out. A woman came running up shouting that there was a monkey ripping up her flat. All I could think was that they had never mentioned monkeys at training school. I let my colleague handle that one.

The increasing demands on our time and the shortage of officers means that we can no longer patrol our beats on foot. Instead, much of the patrolling is done in panda cars, and we all have personal radios so we can be directed where we're needed more quickly. Many of the calls coming over the radio direct you to an address to deal with a 'disturbance', leaving you to find out what the disturbance is. When you get there it may turn out to be a dispute between two people who need help in sorting things out. The problem with many disputes is that if you try and steer a middle course, you are assumed by each side to be biased in favour of the other. Some disputes and emergencies you just can't resolve, and you need to know where to send people so they can get help.

Many criminals are arrested by uniformed officers at the time of the crime or soon afterwards. Often you see something while patrolling that doesn't look quite right, and investigation reveals a thief at work. Often the arrest comes after stopping and searching someone in the street who has aroused your suspicions. I know being stopped and searched can be an unpleasant experience, but the more people co-operate the less unpleasant it is. In my experience, very few people object — they know they have nothing to hide and that we're trying to protect their property as well. However, one area where we can become unpopular is in dealing with offending motorists. No motorist likes being pulled up for a traffic offence and many drivers feel there are so many regulations it is impossible to obey them all.

Another drawback to police duty is that you end up with many of the unpleasant jobs, such as informing someone of the death of a relative. People dread the arrival of the police at the door because it often means bad news.

Chris Steele Perkins

More and more of our time seems to be spent dealing with public order events, like preventing fights at football matches and escorting marches or demonstrations. Our aim is to ensure that these take place with as little interference to normal life as possible. One thing that often worries me is that the more time I spend at demonstrations the less time I can spend with the people who live in the area of my station.

It's unpleasant going on a march knowing that there is to be a counter march, and that we are going to have to keep both sides apart.

But it would be wrong to give the impression that police work is all go. Much of the time is spent on routine patrolling, where nothing out of the ordinary seems to be happening. Of course, you never know how many crimes you have prevented.

Many officers feel isolated from people outside the force, because of the problems of maintaining a regular social life while working shifts. You only get one weekend off in four and that is frequently cancelled because of a demonstration or a football match.

Officers know that their uniform makes them different and that some people will be only too happy to see them make a mistake. I know of one

officer whose father hasn't spoken to him since he joined over five years ago.

With all its problems, I enjoy my job — you really never know what is going to happen next. Even though it has its frustrations, it has its rewards too, not least of all knowing that most of the time you are helping people who need you. I wouldn't change it for the world.

Metropolitan Police

?

1 Why do police officers wear uniforms?

2 Some people argue that the way to improve relations with the police is to put more police on foot and fewer police in cars — what are your views on this suggestion?

3 The officer talking above sees his work as 'helping people who need you'. List some of the jobs that the police do and discuss their order of importance.

4 This officer is concerned about the time he spends at demonstrations. What are your views?

5 List the qualities and abilities that you think a police officer should have, in order of their importance, and compare your list with others in the class.

6 Is it possible for a police officer ever to be really off-duty?

The powers of the police

Some of the main police powers are listed on this page. We have invented some examples of possible situations  for you to discuss.

On arrest

The police can search anyone who has been arrested. If you are arrested at home, your home can also be searched.

For example The police had an arrest warrant for John D. He was found having a meal at a friend's flat. The police searched the flat and then searched other flats nearby. Do you think they should have carried out these searches? Why would they want to do this?

With a warrant

If the police wish to search any premises, they must first obtain a warrant under one of the laws allowing this (for example, The Misuse of Drugs Act). They have to satisfy a magistrate that there are good reasons for a search. In certain circumstances, a police super-intendent will give written authority for a search to take place.

For example A CID officer was informed over the telephone, by a man who refused to give his name, that the landlord of the Dog and Duck pub had received some crates of stolen whisky. He applied to the magistrate for a warrant. If you had been the magistrate, would you have issued it? What further information would you want?

Without a warrant or arrest

The police may search you in public if they have reasonable suspicion that you are carrying stolen property, drugs or firearms, or if they suspect you might be a terrorist.

For example A girl on her way to work, carrying a large handbag, was stopped in the street by two policemen who asked to search her. She asked for the names and numbers of the police officers, what they were looking for, why they were searching her and under what powers. She then insisted on being taken to the police station to be searched by a policewoman. Do you think the officers had to agree to all her requests?

Some police want

They want to be able to stop, search and detain people and search their vehicles at any time, or in any place, to look for offensive weapons, or simply if they believe that this might help to prevent a crime. They also want more power to seize property that they think might be useful as evidence. They would like senior officers to be able to give permission to have road blocks set up.

Arrest

With a warrant

If the police have a good reason to suspect that you have committed a crime, they can ask a magistrate for a warrant to arrest you. They can only apply for a warrant if the offence carries a term of imprisonment, or if they cannot establish your address.

Without a warrant

The police can arrest you if you are found committing, or attempting to commit, any offence which carries a penalty of five years in prison for a first offence (for example, theft). They can also arrest you if they think you are mentally ill and in need of care and control. Some offences with lower penalties, such as conduct likely to cause a breach of the peace, are also cause for arrest.

For example A leading member of an extreme right-wing political group was talking to a large public meeting in the street. After a heated speech about immigration which upset several Asians nearby, he was arrested for using insulting words likely to cause a breach of the peace. Was the arrest lawful, and are there alternative charges that he could have faced? (see page 78).

Detention

You can only be forced to go to the police station if you have been arrested. Of course, you can agree to go to the police station of your own free will. If you have been arrested without a warrant and you are being held in custody for a serious crime, the police must take you before a magistrate as soon as it's practical.

For example Two police officers stopped Alan (aged nineteen) from playing in a children's playground and then asked him to accompany them to the police station. Alan refused. What could the officers do?

Record keeping

If you have been charged with an offence, the police will probably ask to photograph you and take your fingerprints. However, they should not force you to have these things done, unless they are holding you under The Prevention of Terrorism Act. If you refuse to have your fingerprints taken, the police can get a magistrate's permission to compel you to agree. If they get this permission and you are either not charged, or are acquitted, you can insist that your fingerprints are destroyed.

For example The police arrested Jane for shoplifting. At the police station they told her they were going to take her photographs and fingerprints. She refused. What could the police do?

greater powers...

They want the power to arrest any suspect who refuses to give a name and address, or who gives one that they believe to be false.

They want the power to detain a person for up to 72 hours before making charges and to extend detention indefinitely, with a magistrate's permission. They also argue that a prosecutor should have the right to comment in court on people who have exercised their right to remain silent.

They want to be able to compel all people working or living in any particular area to have their fingerprints taken if it would assist in an investigation. They also want to photograph all people who have been charged.

1 Now that you have read about the powers which the police have:
a) which of these do you think should be extended, and which do you think should be reduced?
b) what would be the advantages and disadvantages of extending police powers, both for the public and for the police? Discuss these questions with your group using examples from your own experience, if possible.

2 Are there any powers not mentioned that you think the police should be given?

What would you do?

Listed below are the outline notes of an incident.

• Two police officers in a Rover police car.

• It's 12.02 am — two minutes past midnight.

• It's raining.

• There have already been five calls this evening: housebreaking in a block of flats, a motorbike stolen outside a rowdy teenage party, a domestic dispute (fight between a husband and wife), a false alarm (suspected break-in of warehouse).

• Radio crackles into life and they are called to a disturbance.

• A sixty-mile-an-hour dash to the disturbance, at a local pub.

• When they arrive at the pub there is:
a) a large crowd blocking the street
b) a person badly injured
c) a small group of very angry people
d) a hysterical old man
e) a publican who has been serving drinks after hours
f) a smashed plate-glass window in the pub door

1 Write a story or play describing the incident from the moment it is reported, either from the point of view of one of the police officers in the car, or from the point of view of the publican who was a witness to the whole incident.

2 Imagine the whole incident and report it accurately in a 'police notebook' with all the details which you think will be necessary in court. Add plans and diagrams.

3 Write, discuss, or act out:
a) the discussion that takes place on arrival at the scene of the incident (think hard about what the police will be trying to do)
b) the discussion between the two police officers in the car immediately after the call and as they speed towards the incident

4 Discuss the order in which the police should tackle things when they arrive on the scene of such an incident. What should their priorities be?

5 What do you think are the advantages and disadvantages of being in a high-powered car with a radio, some distance away from the incident?

Imagine you are walking down the street carrying a bag, and suddenly you realise that you have forgotten something. With a look of shock, you turn and rush home. A police officer notices you and decides that your behaviour is reasonable grounds for suspecting you are carrying stolen property. She stops you and insists on searching you.

Many people would feel resentful or angry at this. However, since thieves have to transfer stolen goods to the place where they dispose of or store them, the police argue that their power to search is both a deterrent and a vital way of detecting offenders. But in order to prevent and detect crime, the police need everybody's co-operation, and they may become unpopular by searching innocent people.

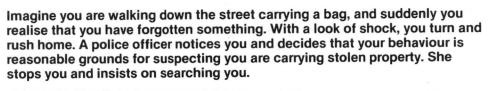

Search

Search without a warrant

The police have the power to search for stolen property, drugs, firearms and evidence of terrorism.

Two policemen decided to stop a green estate car. When they searched it, they found a blanket in the boot, and underneath the blanket they discovered a safe. The driver of the car was taking it home in order to open it. In a court of law, the man was found guilty of burglary.

Search with a warrant

Any search must be thorough; however, compensation may sometimes be paid for property damaged during a search.

A man was remanded on a charge of theft. The police went to his house with a search warrant which stated that they were looking for cash or silver. It was just before Christmas. In the search, the police officers looked in all possible hiding places, including the children's Christmas presents, but found nothing. Later the man was charged for a post office theft.

Search on arrest

When people are arrested, the police are entitled to search them. In certain circumstances, if, for example, the police suspect the presence of drugs, this can include a 'body search' — an uncomfortable and embarrassing experience. It includes a search of the vagina, the anus and the cavities of the teeth.

The drug squad raided a pub and made a mass arrest of young people. A woman was one of the 32 stripped and searched at the local police station after the raid. A police woman examined her internally wearing a pair of unsterilised gloves. The search failed to turn up any drugs. No one was charged.

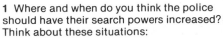

1 Where and when do you think the police should have their search powers increased? Think about these situations:
● at a football match
● at school
● getting on an aeroplane
● in an art gallery
● in a pub
● at a demonstration
● on the streets

Think about some other situations with your group.

2 Do you think the police should have their search powers controlled?

Discuss this with your group and give reasons for your decision.

Every day a number of people are arrested by the police, and many others are summoned to appear in court on different charges. Sometimes the arrest is by warrant issued to the police. With a warrant they can enter premises forcibly, if necessary, to make an arrest. In other cases, individual police officers have to make on-the-spot decisions about whether or not to make an arrest.

Arrest and detention

After arrest, suspects are taken to the police station and allowed to ask for someone to be told of their arrest and their whereabouts as soon as possible. They are then searched and interviewed. An arrested person has certain basic rights. One is to keep silent. People are often frightened when they are at the police station and it is easy to say something that might be misleading or misunderstood. It's usually better to say nothing until you've talked to a lawyer.

When interviewing suspects, the police are expected to conform to **The Judges' Rules.** These are recommendations only, not law. If you are arrested, 'The Judges' Rules recommend that:

● you should be able to contact and talk to a solicitor privately
● you should be made reasonably comfortable
● if you are under seventeen, the police should tell your parents or guardian of the arrest, and you should not be interviewed unless a parent or another adult of the same sex as yourself (other than a police officer) is present

If the police do not obey these rules, they may find that the evidence they present is not allowed in court, or the individual can make a complaint, probably through a solicitor, to the police chief of the area. If the police decide to lay a charge, things should proceed as shown opposite.

Taking fingerprints

Everybody's fingerprints are different. With your teacher's permission, compare the fingerprints of the class. You will need: sheets of glossy paper; newspaper; a soft paint-brush; a spatula and carbon powder. (Perhaps your local toy shop or your school's science department could help.)

A Lay the newspaper on the table, place a piece of glossy paper on top and press your finger hard on to it to make a fingerprint.

B Sprinkle a small amount of carbon powder on to the fingerprint.

C Gently brush off the carbon powder.

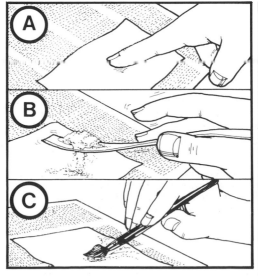

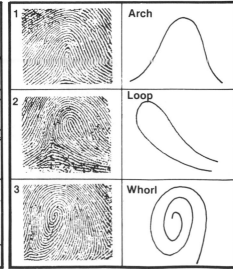

The station officer is told about the arrest, to make sure the charge is correct.

The station officer tells the prisoner of her rights and asks if she has anything to say.

The prisoner is searched and charge forms are prepared.

She signs a form which correctly lists her property.

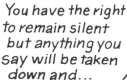

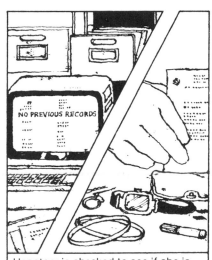

She is charged and given a copy of the charge. If she agrees, her fingerprints and photographs are taken.

She is put in a cell.

Her story is checked to see if she is known or wanted by the police. If eligible, she is bailed. Then her property is checked against the list and returned to her.

She is released on bail. This means she can go free until the date of the court hearing — but the police may impose conditions.

1 Take the fingerprints of your class, and classify them into the three main groups. Which group is the most common? A fingerprint with several patterns is called a composite print. Remember to destroy the fingerprints you have taken!

2 Using all the information on this page, write and design a poster or a leaflet for teenagers, giving advice to them on what they should expect and what they should do if they are arrested.

3 On these pages you have read how individuals are charged at a police station. Now discuss the following:

a) The Judges' Rules are designed to ensure that any statement made by an accused person and offered in evidence has been obtained voluntarily. What penalties could be imposed on the police who break these rules? Do you think they should become law?

b) Should conversations between the police and suspects be tape-recorded or videotaped? What are the advantages, and what could be the disadvantages?

c) Should there be a fixed period of time after which police must release detainees if they have not been charged?

d) Police have the right to question any individual who they believe can assist them with their enquiries. Should they also have the power to detain these people for questioning?

4 Do you think everybody's fingerprints should be available to the police to assist them in catching criminals?

Today, personal information about people is gradually becoming more easily available. More and more details are being put on computers, and centralised to make finding out easier. Banks, the civil service, insurance companies, the social services, the Inland Revenue, employers and the police all have stores of information on people, and this information can be passed on.

Information

Police records

The police collect information on all sorts of people: people who have been arrested, criminals, people who have reported crimes, witnesses to crime, people who have made complaints about the police and people who the police believe are likely to commit crimes in the future. This information is stored in a number of ways:
● in the Police National Computer at Hendon, which holds over 30 million entries. This is linked to every police station in the country by a visual display unit (VDU)
● in other computers
● in card-index systems
● in files

Great care is said to be taken to stop people outside the police force getting information, but in 1976

The Times newspaper reported that people could obtain information over the phone, by posing as police officers.

Local authority social services departments ask the police to check if people who want to be foster parents or to adopt children are known to have anything in their past which would make them unsuitable.

Also, certain people employed in youth work, the civil service, medicine, teaching, atomic energy and the Post Office can expect information about any convictions to be passed on to their employers by the police.

In 1979 the *Guardian* discovered that 93 possible jury members were being vetted, using police records, before a political trial. This discovery caused a great deal of concern.

What the police computer said about 19 jurors

Not only people with minor criminal records are listed, but those whose family and friends have records. People who complain about the police; who have children the police have charged but failed to convict; have expired convictions under the Rehabilitation of Offenders Act; or people who have been the victims of crime — all these have been logged on the police computers, and the information passed on to the barristers and the defence.

Other records, too, can seriously affect your future.

Your file may contain information which is inaccurate, incomplete, out-of-date or irrelevant.

For example During the three months since he had left school, David had applied unsuccessfully for many jobs. Finally, at one interview, the employer told him that his record from school said 'David is a thief'. The previous term David had been accused of stealing by one of his classmates. However, he had an alibi for the time of the theft and, after investigation, the headteacher had admitted his innocence. David saw the headteacher and the record was altered.

The information you give for one purpose may be transferred, without your knowledge and consent, for an entirely different purpose.

For example The Vehicle Registration and Licensing Index in Swansea is a computerised record of all people in Britain who own vehicles. This information is automatically transferred to the Police National Computer at Hendon, and up-to-date addresses are passed on to the Inland Revenue who use them for chasing tax evaders. It takes only seconds to check the owner of a given vehicle licence number.

Other people may be able to see information which you thought was confidential.

For example Every ten years there is a compulsory census, when people are obliged by law to fill in personal details on a form. The information collected is confidential for 100 years after its collection and the staff involved are sworn to secrecy.

In 1971, one of the enumerators (people working on the census) noticed that one of the houses he visited to collect the form was being used for business purposes and not just as a residence. He mentioned this at work in his local rating department.

As a result, he was prosecuted, and found guilty of disclosing confidential information. He was fined £20, and it was made clear that he was unlikely to be employed as an enumerator again.

Information may be collected without your knowledge and consent.

For example If you want to buy something on hire purchase, the company you apply to for credit will check your credit-worthiness through a central register. Apart from other things, this will tell them if you have ever failed to repay a debt. You may never know that this has happened or how much information was available to them.

1 Listed opposite are some of the main agencies which collect and store information. Do you think that this information should be available to anyone who wants it, including yourself?

2 What remedies, if any, should be available to enable individuals to correct errors in their own records?

3 Keeping records helps the police to fight crime and protect your interests.
a) What sort of information do you think the police should keep?
b) Do you think the information should be controlled and, if so, how?
c) Should any information be taken off the computer after a certain period of time?
d) Who should police information be available to?
e) Should people have the right to see their own records?

The arms of the law

The popular image of the local bobby doing his rounds on his bike has changed in recent years, with the appearance of armed officers in situations like the Balcombe Street siege or the siege at the Iranian Embassy.

J. Pick

Should our police be armed?

The police always have access to arms and to trained marksmen, but they are still opposed to carrying guns on normal duty, both as a force and as individuals. As one police officer said: 'We don't want anyone flaunting guns in public, whoever they are.' However, the increased rate of armed crime and terrorism means that there is a greater risk of the police coming up against armed criminals when they themselves are unarmed.

Some people argue that armed officers might be a greater deterrent to criminals, and that officers would be better protected if they carried guns.

Others argue that if police were armed on duty, criminals might react by carrying guns more frequently. There would be a greater chance of accidental injury, both to the public and the police. If they were armed, the police would be less approachable and more isolated from the public. Some recruits might even join the police force just to carry guns.

Despite these arguments, guns were issued to the police on 12 114 occasions during 1976 and 1977. In 1978 alone, guns were issued on 7462 occasions and in the first ten months of 1979 guns were issued on 5614 occasions. London has over 200 armed members of the Special Patrol Group and 15 per cent of all police have been through a firearms training course.

Discuss the following questions with your group.

1 In some countries all police are permanently armed. Would you like to see this in Britain?

2 What do you think are the dangers associated with the police using firearms?

The private security industry

Securicor

There are about 400 private security firms in Britain. The biggest is Securicor, which employs 23 000 men. Many of their duties involve policing, and many of them are ex-policemen. They transport money and goods, and provide guards and guard dogs for premises. Some firms give advice on security and install radio systems to protect lorries from being hijacked. Security firms guard airports, warehouses, offices and stores, and some operate security checks at airports. Many provide store detectives or personal bodyguards. They investigate theft, sometimes by working under cover. Security firms have been used by employers on lockouts (where employers refuse entry to workers); and some undertake industrial spying.

Guards drive armoured trucks and cars. Firms maintain guarded storerooms, some of which are nuclear-proof.

Because of their uniforms, people may confuse private security guards with the police. Some firms have been prosecuted for providing uniforms too similar to those of the police.

Some police officers welcome private security firms, feeling that they do vital work which could not be done by the force without more officers. Others believe that these firms should be subject to stricter controls since they operate for profit rather than for the good of the public.

Securicor

What would you do?

Should private security firms be better controlled? Divide into groups and make up some rules for the operation of private security firms. Each group should take one of the problems below.

1 Should guards wear uniforms, and should these be allowed to look like police uniforms?

2 Should guards be allowed to carry guns and, if so, on what occasions? How would you check that they obey your rules?

3 Should ex-police officers be allowed to work for private security firms and, if so, how could you control information about people's records passing between police officers and ex-police officers?

4 Should private security firms be involved in checking up on theft by workers in factories, or used by employers in strikes and lockouts?

The groups should write down or report verbally on their conclusions, with reasons.

39

COUNTY OF LANCASTER CONSTABULARY FORCE.

THE FOLLOWING MAXIMS

Are to be strictly observed and borne in mind by the Constables of the Force

1. Constables are placed in authority to PROTECT, not to OPPRESS, the PUBLIC.

2. To do which effectually, they must earnestly and systematically exert themselves to PREVENT CRIME.

3. When a Crime has been committed, no time should be lost, nor exertions spared, to discover and bring to justice the OFFENDERS.

4. Obtain a knowledge of all REPUTED THIEVES, and IDLE and DISORDERLY PERSONS.

5. Watch narrowly all Persons having NO VISIBLE MEANS OF SUBSISTENCE.

6. Prevent VAGRANCY.

7. Be IMPARTIAL in the discharge of duties.

8. Discard from the mind all POLITICAL and SECTARIAN prejudices.

9. Be COOL and INTREPID in the discharge of duties in emergencies and unavoidable conflicts.

10. Avoid ALTERCATIONS, and display PERFECT COMMAND of TEMPER under INSULT and gross PROVOCATION, to which all Constables must occasionally be liable.

11. NEVER STRIKE but in SELF-DEFENCE, nor treat a Prisoner with more Rigour than may be absolutely necessary to prevent escape.

12. Practice the most complete SOBRIETY, one instance of DRUNKENNESS will render a Constable liable to DISMISSAL.

13. Treat with the utmost CIVILITY all classes of HER MAJESTY'S SUBJECTS, and cheerfully render ASSISTANCE to all in need of it.

14. Exhibit DEFERENCE and RESPECT to the MAGISTRACY.

15. Promptly and cheerfully OBEY all SUPERIOR OFFICERS.

16. Render an HONEST, FAITHFUL, and SPEEDY account of all MONIES and PROPERTY, whether intrusted with them for others, or taken possession of in the execution of duty.

17. With reference to the foregoing, bear especially in mind that "HONESTY IS THE BEST POLICY."

18. Be perfectly neat and clean in Person and Attire.

19. Never sit down in a PUBLIC HOUSE or BEER SHOP.

20. AVOID TIPPLING.

21. It is the interest of every man to devote some portion of his spare time to the practice of READING and WRITING and the general improvement of his mind.

22. IGNORANCE is an insuperable bar to promotion.

J. WOODFORD

Chief Constable

Courts, Crime

& Punishment

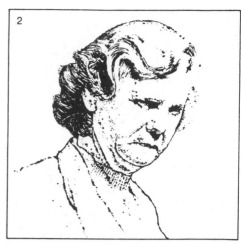

The true story of Luke Dougherty

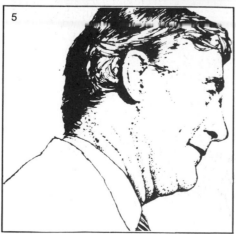

The characters

1 Mr Butterfield: manager of the store
2 Miss Mallin: shop assistant
3 PC Anderson
4 Mrs Hall: Luke Dougherty's friend
5 Mr Hamilton: solicitor
6 WPC Stephenson
7 Mr Fenwick: barrister
8 Judge Gill: the Crown Court judge
9 Mrs Thoms: coach trip organiser
10 Mr Briggs: legal secretary, *Justice*
11 Robert Carr: Home Secretary at the time
12 Luke Dougherty with his children

A fuller version of the events reported here can be found in the *Report to the Secretary of State for the Home Department of the Departmental Committee on Evidence of Identification in Criminal Cases* (Chairman: Right Hon Lord Devlin), 1976, HMSO, known more commonly as the Devlin Report. Items in quotation marks are taken verbatim from this report.

To answer some of the questions in this section, you will need to refer to pages 52 to 66.

AUG 23 1972

In a store in Sunderland, just after 11.30 am, a group of people — a youth, a man and an elderly woman with a limp — were seen stealing some curtains. The manager, Mr Butterfield, followed the man, who was carrying the bag, outside and asked him to return to the store. On their way back, the man swung the door hard on Mr Butterfield and ran out of another door, leaving the bag. Inside were three sets of curtains valued at £11.25.

PC Anderson was sent to investigate. He talked to Mr Butterfield and took a description of the man as 'aged approximately 55 years, 5ft 8ins tall, ginger hair cut short, well-built, wearing glasses, dark green-brown coat.' Although Miss Mallin, the shop assistant, had seen the man, the officer didn't ask her for a description. He was told about the other two suspects and given their descriptions, but he didn't note this down or report it.

Theft

The theft

The escape

PC Anderson questions Mr Butterfield

?

1 Do you know why Mr Butterfield allowed the shoplifters to leave the shop before stopping them?

2 Do you think that PC Anderson recorded all that he should? What further questions would you have asked if you had been there?

AUG 24 1972 Mr Butterfield and Miss Mallin arrived at the police station, and together they looked at photographs of convicted criminals. They picked out one of Luke Dougherty. He was aged 43, 5ft 5ins tall, with black hair. Dougherty. . . 'had a long career of petty crime, mostly dishonesty.'

 SEPT 6 1972 PC Anderson went to see Luke Dougherty, and told him that he was suspected of shoplifting on 23 August. He took Luke Dougherty with him to the police station, where he was cautioned. Dougherty said that he knew nothing of the theft, but he couldn't remember where he was when it happened. He agreed to appear in an identification parade.

Mr Butterfield and Miss Mallin were called to view the identification parade, but Luke Dougherty didn't appear and the police couldn't get enough volunteers to take part. The parade was cancelled. Next day Luke Dougherty was arrested.

He protested that he had made a mistake about the date of the identification parade, but he was charged with the theft of the curtains, released on bail, and told to appear at the Magistrates' Court on 18 October.

When Luke Dougherty returned home, he was reminded by his friend, Mrs Hall, that on 23 August they had taken his four children on a coach trip to Whitley Bay. The coach left at about 11.50 am, and Luke Dougherty had met Mrs Hall at 11.30 am. So he had an alibi — he was waiting for the coach at the time of the robbery.

Identification

The witnesses look at police files

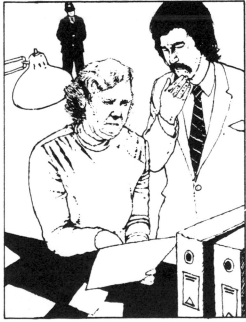

Luke Dougherty is arrested

He remembers the coach trip

?

1 Should Miss Mallin and Mr Butterfield have seen the police photographs together?

2 What was Luke Dougherty's alibi? If you were defending Luke Dougherty, what would you need to do to make the alibi stronger? How would you get this information?

3 What were the differences between Mr Butterfield's description of the thief and Luke Dougherty?

4 Think of a date about a month ago. Can you give a very detailed explanation of where you were, what you wore, and what you were doing on that day?

5 As a group, act out an incident in front of another group who should then relate this as if to the police, with accurate descriptions of the people involved.

Luke Dougherty discussed the case and the alibi with his solicitor, Mr Hamilton. He thought that the 40 people on the bus could be called as witnesses, but Mr Hamilton said that five or six would be enough, and emphasised that any witnesses must be of good character.

 OCT 18 1972 Luke Dougherty appeared before the magistrates and pleaded not guilty. He elected to go for trial by jury rather than being judged by the magistrates, and was remanded on bail until the committal proceedings. Unknown to him, Mr Butterfield and Miss Mallin were there, saw him and heard him plead not guilty.

NOV 10 1972 At the committal proceedings, Luke Dougherty was ordered to appear at Durham Crown Court for trial on 22 February 1973.
Meanwhile, Mr Hamilton sent the names and addresses of five alibi witnesses to the police prosecutor.

However, he hadn't chosen the witnesses who might have remembered Luke Dougherty best — people who had seen him waiting for the bus, and others who sat near him on the trip and ate with him. Since there was only one other man on the bus (the other passengers were women and children) Luke Dougherty should have been easily remembered.

DEC 12 1972 WPC Stephenson was told to investigate the alibi and interviewed the witnesses. Mrs Thoms, the tour organiser, could not attend the court hearing because she had to take her sick baby to hospital. She understood from WPC Stephenson that she need not worry, as her statement would be read out in court.

Magistrates' Court

Luke Dougherty talks to his solicitor

At the Magistrates' Court

Mrs Thoms is interviewed

?

1 Before you read more of the Luke Dougherty story, look at the magistrate's statement on page 54.
a) What qualities and abilities do you think a magistrate should have?

b) JPs are recruited from local people who are not legally trained or qualified. What are the advantages and disadvantages of this system?

2 Why, in your opinion, did Luke Dougherty choose to go for trial by jury?

3 In a situation where it was possible to select from a large number of witnesses, how would you decide which ones to choose?

Luke Dougherty went to Durham with only three witnesses, as one had failed to turn up that morning. Mr Fenwick, the barrister handling Luke Dougherty's defence in court, conferred with him. One of the alibi witnesses had a criminal record and he decided not to call her. That left only two witnesses: the other man on the coach trip, Mr Pearson, and Mrs Hall. Despite this Mr Fenwick was not too concerned, because he felt that the prosecution's case against Luke Dougherty was weak:
•Luke Dougherty had agreed to attend an identification parade, but none seemed to have been held
•both witnesses who identified Luke Dougherty had previously been shown police photographs
•only one witness had described the thief at the time of the robbery and the colour of hair mentioned was different from Luke Dougherty's.

The police intended to hold a dock identification by asking Miss Mallin and Mr Butterfield to identify the man in the dock as the thief. However, Mr Fenwick felt that, if there was any similarity between the thief and the man in the dock, just seeing him in the dock would convince the witnesses that he was the guilty party they had seen in the store. And if they had seen a photograph of the accused man and then saw him in the dock, they might remember the man they'd studied in the photo rather than the man they'd only glimpsed briefly at the time of the crime. Since this was just what had happened with Mr Butterfield and Miss Mallin, Mr Fenwick could discredit their identification. However, he had a problem: if he told the jury that the witnesses had been shown photos, they would realise that Luke Dougherty had a criminal record, and this might influence their decision.

Defence

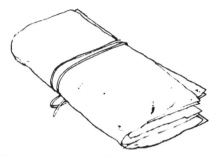

Luke Dougherty and witnesses go to Durham

Mr Fenwick _____ in court

He decides not to call one witness

?

1 How could Luke Dougherty's alibi have been made more convincing to the court? Who could have helped him make it so?

2 How reliable are people's memories about personal appearance? Think of someone all the people in your class or group know well.

Each write a full description of him or her, then compare what you have written. What similarities and differences are there between the descriptions? What reasons may explain why people sometimes give very different accounts of the same person or incident?

FEB 22 1973

The jury was sworn in and Luke Dougherty was formally charged with theft. The jury went out while Mr Fenwick argued that the judge should refuse a dock identification. The judge decided that Luke Dougherty should leave the dock and sit with the jurors, and that Mr Butterfield and Miss Mallin would then be asked to identify the thief from those in the courtroom. No one in court realised that they had already seen him in the dock in the Magistrates' Court. Also, the two witnesses were able to see him through a glass door as he was placed among the jurors. So when they were called in, Mr Butterfield and Miss Mallin both identified Luke Dougherty as the thief.

The two alibi witnesses were called to give evidence. However, the jury knew that there had originally been five witnesses for the defence, and that one of the two now being called, Mrs Hall, was a close friend of Luke Dougherty. Mr Fenwick was given the opportunity to adjourn the hearing to contact more witnesses, but he decided to continue.

Judge Gill told the jury to approach the evidence of identification very carefully, and that dock identification

Crown Court

The witnesses glimpse Luke Dougherty

COURT No 3

Luke Dougherty seated among the jury

He is identified by the witnesses

?

1 Why do you think Mr Fenwick tried to persuade the judge not to allow a dock identification?

2 Why was it so easy for Mr Butterfield and Miss Mallin to identify Luke Dougherty?

3 Why, in your opinion, did Mr Fenwick advise Luke Dougherty not to ask for an adjournment in order to call more alibi witnesses? Do you think this was wise?

4 Using the information in the story and the magistrate's statement on page 54, list the differences between the Magistrates' Court and the Crown Court.

was dangerous. However, after two hours, they returned a unanimous verdict of guilty. The judge gave a six-month sentence and, as Luke Dougherty already had two suspended sentences, said that they should take effect too, making fifteen months in all.

When Mrs Thoms read about the trial, she was shocked. She went to the police to protest and was referred to Mr Hamilton, but the legal aid granted to Luke Dougherty had come to an end, and the solicitor would no longer carry out any work for which he wouldn't be paid. Mrs Thoms also wrote to the *Sunday People*.

Verdict

Bus-trip alibi of father in jail

NEIGHBOURS of labourer Luke Dougherty, now serving 15 months in jail, have started a campaign to free him. They claim he could not have committed the store theft which put him in jail.

The key to his innocence, they say, is a day trip to the seaside she organised last August 23 for local Sunderland children.

On that day, a man dashed from a Sunderland store after being spotted putting curtains worth £11 in a shopping bag. Later Mr Dougherty, 43, was charged with the theft, timed by police as between midday and 12.15 p.m.

But, says Mrs. Th[...]

BID TO FREE ALIBI MAN

LUKE DOUGHERTY has served seven months in jail for a theft he never committed, officials of Justice, the British section of the International Commission of Jurists, claim.

Their chairman, Lord Gardiner, the former Lord Chancellor, is making a direct approach to the Lord Chief Justice and to the Home Office for the immediate release of 43-year-old Mr. Dougherty, of Laurence Court, Sunderland.

Seven months ago the Sunday People spotlighted the case when Dougherty was jailed by Durham Crown Court for six months and ordered to serve a nine-month suspended sentence for a previous offence.

Neighbours of the jailed man wrote to the Sunday People to protest that he could not have committed the theft.

Campaign leader Mrs. Sheila Thoms, 27, said that on the day of the store theft she organised a children's trip to the seaside and that Mr. Dougherty, a labourer, went on it with four of his children.

The verdict of the jury

Luke Dougherty goes to prison

Mrs Thoms reads about the case

1 In any trial of this kind there is a case for the defence and a case for the prosecution. Write down what you think was the case for the defence of Luke Dougherty, and what was the case for his prosecution.

2 List the things that you think went wrong with the case.

3 Using the information on page 57 see if you can find out:
a) who is not allowed to sit on a jury
b) how many jurors must agree on a verdict for it to stand
c) whether the jury are paid
d) what 'suspended sentence' means

MAR 6 1973 Mr Fenwick hadn't liked the way the dock identification was handled, and he applied for permission to appeal against the conviction. Meanwhile, Mrs Thoms contacted *Justice,* an association concerned with the fair operation of the law. In April, Mr Briggs, *Justice's* legal secretary, wrote to the Registrar of Criminal Appeals enclosing a letter from Mrs Thoms, and asked that legal aid be given to pay a solicitor to get further statements, but the Registrar refused.

 MAY 9 1973 The application for leave to appeal was first considered by one judge. He agreed that it should be sent to the Full Court of Appeal who would hear the barrister argue the case, and he granted legal aid for this only. He didn't think it was necessary to call fresh evidence. In the meantime, *Justice* sent a questionnaire to the people on the bus and received ten replies saying Luke Dougherty had been there on that day. Mr Briggs sent these to Mr Fenwick, pointing out the need for a solicitor to take statements. Mr Fenwick wrote to the Registrar, saying that, if Luke Dougherty wished to appeal on the grounds of this fresh evidence, he must have a solicitor to advise him, and a new barrister.

 JUNE 18 1973 The Registrar wrote to Mr Fenwick saying that no further legal aid was available to pay for a solicitor to help Luke Dougherty, but that Mr Fenwick could draw the Court's attention to the new evidence. He also wrote to Luke Dougherty in prison explaining that Mr Fenwick would only be able to appeal on the question of identification, and would not be able to apply for leave to call new witnesses. He also pointed out that if Luke Dougherty didn't want Mr Fenwick to handle the appeal, there would be a long delay while another barrister was brought in. Luke Dougherty replied 'I have all faith in my barrister and accept that he handles my case in Full Court without any witnesses being present.'

Campaign

Mr Briggs writes to the registrar

Mr Fenwick argues the case

The judges dismiss the application

1 Mr Fenwick was not allowed by law to bring evidence at an appeal that had been available but was not cited at the original trial. How did this lessen Luke Dougherty's chances of winning his case?

2 Why, in your opinion, did Luke Dougherty decide that Mr Fenwick should appeal on his behalf?

3 Read through the case again and imagine you are running the campaign to free Luke Dougherty. How would you organise your campaign?

JULY 12 1973

In court, Mr Fenwick argued the case, on the grounds that dock identification was unsatisfactory. The Court dismissed the application for an appeal although they knew about the new witnesses. Luke Dougherty was taken to the Court of Appeal building but was not called in to the courtroom or visited by his barrister.

Mrs Thoms went on with her campaign. She wrote to her MP and so did Luke Dougherty. On 21 October there was another article in the *Sunday People.* However, 'the most effective action came from *Justice.*' They instructed a solicitor to take as many statements as possible from the people in the bus party. The solicitor made a report which included thirteen statements. He felt that these left Luke Dougherty's conviction 'open to the gravest challenge' and *Justice* sent a memorandum to the Home Secretary.

NOV 6 1973

The Home Secretary sent this material from *Justice* to the Chief Constable of Durham, urgently requesting a brief report. The Chief Constable replied that if the evidence supplied by *Justice* had been available earlier, Dougherty probably would not have been charged. The Chief Constable called for an enquiry by an officer from another force.

NOV 14 1973

The Home Secretary sent the case back to the Court of Appeal. The Court ordered Luke Dougherty's immediate release on bail (he was due to be released on 21 December). The Court of Appeal directed that the new evidence be taken to court. This eventually took place in February 1974 with Luke Dougherty represented by a new barrister and solicitor. After a number of witnesses had been heard, the prosecution decided not to oppose the appeal.

MAR 14 1974

The appeal was heard. The Lord Chief Justice gave the judgement of the court: 'A very large number of statements have been obtained, all of which go to show that Mr Dougherty was on the bus in question and was not committing an offence. . . as alleged and . . . the appeal will be allowed: the conviction is quashed.'

JAN 21 1975

Mr Dougherty was paid £2000 compensation by the Home Office for his wrongful conviction and its consequences.

Appeal

The Home Secretary considers the case

Luke Dougherty is freed

1 Imagine you are a newspaper reporter in court when the appeal is heard. Write a report, bearing in mind that the readers will have no knowledge of the background to the case.

2 Using the information on page 55:
a) when and against what can a convicted person appeal?
b) describe how an appeal is made
c) describe the work of the Home Secretary and find out who the Home Secretary is now.

Who's who in the legal world

The Solicitor

If you need to contact a solicitor, check with friends to see if they can recommend anyone or contact your local Citizens' Advice Bureau or law centre. There are also lists of solicitors in your local library and in the *Yellow Pages*.

❝ You may not realise how often I can give help, or that my services can often be given free or very cheaply indeed. For both criminal and civil matters (see page 53) there is a legal aid system. You pay me little or nothing; and I am paid later (the money comes from taxes).

If you know the police want to question you, contact me first so that I can be present when you are interviewed.

If you have been arrested, you have the right to make a telephone call to a friend or a solicitor. If you phone a friend, ask him or her to get you a solicitor. I can make phone calls to the police and also come along to the police station when necessary to shorten the time you are kept in police custody.

If you have to go to court accused of a criminal offence, I can help in a number of ways.

If you are innocent, I can take down details of your story and also interview others who may be able to show that what you are saying is true. I can then go to court and explain your story. If the case is in a Magistrates' Court I can speak for you personally; if it is more serious, and has to be dealt with by the Crown Court, I will get a barrister to speak for you.

If you are not sure how far I can help you in any particular situation, it is worth telephoning me and making an appointment. Often I can give you advice at an early stage which may prevent you from being misled. **❞**

The Barrister

Training to be a barrister takes at least four and a half years. Barristers, like solicitors, usually take a three-year law degree. Then they take a nine-month course with a final examination which qualifies them to be called to the bar.

❝ When I appear in the higher courts, like the Crown Court, I have to wear a wig and gown. Some say it is important to keep the traditional dress and the pomp and ceremony of the courts in order to demonstrate the seriousness of the law; others say it is unnecessary and divorces barristers and judges from real people and real problems. They argue that if wigs are not used in some courts, like the Magistrates' and Juvenile Courts, they are not necessary at all.

Most of my job, wig or no wig, is speaking in public on behalf of a client — cross-examining witnesses, addressing a jury, arguing points of law or trying to persuade the judge to be lenient in passing sentence. Many people ask how I can defend somebody I know to be guilty. The answer is simple: I don't. If he tells me he is guilty he must either plead guilty (and I will speak for him) or get another barrister. If he denies the offence I must fight the case. He may be lying, or he may be innocent. The court, not the barrister, decides the truth. My job is to do the best for my client.

One of the worst parts of the job is going to see a client in the court cells when a sentence of prison or borstal has just been passed. Some are used to the gates shutting behind them, but others are shocked and frightened, suddenly cut off from the outside world, their friends and families.

Not all my work concerns criminal cases. Individuals or companies may want to sue in the civil courts. If successful, they can recover damages, for example for breach of contract, or for personal injuries suffered at work or in a road accident, or for an unpaid debt.

Nearly everything in our lives is affected by the law. If something goes wrong connected with housing, employment or marriage, we may have to go to court about it. But many civil cases settle out of court when the parties reach an agreement. My work in this involves drafting formal documents and giving written advice on points of law and the chances of success in fighting or defending a particular case.

Some barristers specialise in other fields of law such as tax, shipping or European law. But the majority of the 5000 barristers in England and Wales do a mixture of criminal and general civil cases. That's what I do. It's hard work and I don't always win, but I enjoy it. **❞**

The Judge

Most judges have trained and practised as barristers before appointment by the Lord Chancellor. They are paid a salary and a pension. They must retire at the age of 70.

❝ A High Court judge has many different tasks — this is why my job is so interesting. What you see is the work done in court, but there is a great deal more besides — reading case papers, preparing judgements and summings up, dealing with applications to the Parole Board, to mention only a few.

I spend half my working life 'on circuit', trying cases in the provincial Crown Courts, and the other half at the Royal Courts of Justice or the Old Bailey, in London. I take my turn at sitting in the Court of Appeal (Criminal Division).

Conducting a case in court is not easy. Each party has a Counsel to put the case. I sit back and listen, but I must intervene if Counsel is being irrelevant or is not following the proper rules. I must keep my intervention to the minimum: it is very difficult for Counsel to develop the case properly before a judge who keeps interrupting.

I have to make sure that the jury understands what the witness is saying. I know what the prosecution case is, but not what the defence may be, and it is often difficult to decide what is relevant. But it is vital to make sure that the jury are following closely because it is they, and not me, who will make the decision.

At the end of the case I sum up. This is a difficult and important task. I have to direct the jury fully as to the legal principles which they must follow. I have to sum up the facts and yet make it clear to the jury that the responsibility for deciding questions of fact is theirs alone. I must piece the evidence together so as to direct the jury's minds to the questions to be decided, without making any attempt to suggest what the answer should be.

If there is a verdict of guilty, I pass sentence. I am provided with a good deal of material as to the defendant's circumstances and hear a plea in mitigation. I ask myself whether the normal penalty must apply or whether there are grounds for leniency.

In a judge's life scarcely a day goes by without some new problem emerging. The search for a just solution is fascinating and rewarding. **"**

The Magistrate

There are two kinds of magistrates — **stipendiary magistrates** who are full-time, paid, trained lawyers: they work in large cities where the number of cases daily is very high; and **Justices of the Peace,** who are unpaid, local people who are prepared to give up time or can be released from their jobs to try minor cases in court. There are over 24,000 magistrates in England and Wales.

All magistrates are appointed by the Lord Chancellor on behalf of the Queen. If the area is a county, the recommendation is made by the Lord Lieutenant of the county (who may, of course, be a woman) with the help of an advisory committee. If the area is a large town, the recommendation is made by the advisory committee only. Anyone can be nominated to be a magistrate: often political organisations make nominations. These are discussed by an advisory committee made up of local people.

" I have been a JP for two years. There are always other magistrates present on the bench — the maximum number is seven, but the usual number is three. The court's main function is as a court of trial where criminal offences are tried. There are two types of criminal offence: **summary** offences and **indictable** offences.

A summary offence is one which can be tried in a Magistrates' Court but if it carries a penalty of more than three months in prison, the accused has the right to a trial by jury. Summary offences include most motoring offences such as driving without due care, or driving under the influence of drink. Other offences such as vandalism, causing a disturbance, or being drunk and disorderly are also tried summarily.

Indictable offences are more serious and are usually dealt with in a Crown Court. Under certain circumstances the accused may be given a choice between trial by jury in the Crown Court or by magistrates locally. Theft is an indictable offence with a maximum penalty of several years' imprisonment.

Our other important function is to carry out preliminary investigations called **committal proceedings.** When someone accused of an indictable offence chooses to go before a jury in a Crown Court, we have to investigate the circumstances to see whether the prosecution has enough evidence to make a trial worthwhile. We have no authority to give a verdict on these cases.

In addition to this, we also hear civil cases, like matrimonial orders for separation or maintenance and a variety of other cases, including administering the licensing laws. Our jurisdiction in civil cases is very limited and these cases are fewer in number. **"**

Leave to appeal

The Court of Appeal (Criminal Division)

Justice

You have a right to apply for leave to appeal from the Crown Court, either against conviction or sentence or against both, but your appeal may be turned down. The notice of appeal is examined by a single judge, who may allow your appeal to go on to the Full Court — or may reject your application.

The Court of Appeal (Criminal Division) can only correct mistakes in the law made by judges, or reduce excessive sentences. The Court can receive fresh evidence if they think it necessary. One of the conditions for their accepting this evidence is that it must either have been unavailable at the time of the trial, or kept back for some good reason.

If leave to appeal is refused by the single judge or the Full Court, the only way to reopen a case is by petitioning the Home Secretary with fresh evidence. But it is very rare for a case to be referred back to the Appeal Court by the Home Secretary.

Justice is an organisation concerned with law reform. Its members are from all branches of the legal profession — barristers, solicitors and teachers of law. Its main concerns are to ensure that the law operates fairly, and to press for improvements — for example in the criminal appeal system.

From time to time *Justice* helps prisoners who claim that they have been wrongly convicted to appeal or petition the Home Secretary.

Justice also helps with complaints against government departments and local authority councils. It pressed for the appointment of an **ombudsman** — an official appointed to investigate complaints against these bodies. An ombudsman can, of course, be a woman.

The Home Secretary

The Home Secretary is a Member of Parliament and a high-ranking member of the Cabinet, appointed by the Prime Minister. He or she presides over the Home Office, which deals with immigration, race relations, equal opportunities, crime, the police, prisons, and petitions from prisoners. The Home Secretary appoints the Metropolitan Commissioner of Police, and has overall command of police for the London area. He or she can initiate research into all these areas and can also order inquiries.

Innocent till proved guilty

In England and Wales it is the job of the police to detect crime and catch people suspected of crime. It is the job of the courts to try those suspects.

The rights of the accused

☞ A person is assumed to be innocent until proved guilty. If kept in prison **on remand** (in custody while further evidence is being obtained) before trial, the accused has more rights than convicted prisoners.

☞ The prosecution must prove the charge it is making against the accused. It must first prove that a crime has been committed, then that the accused is guilty.

☞ Proof must be beyond all reasonable doubt. It is thought better not to convict at all than to convict a person who could be innocent.

☞ The trial must be held in public, except in juvenile court cases, where it is held in private to protect children and their families.

☞ Witnesses must give evidence in the presence of the accused, and the accused must be allowed to question them when they have given their evidence.

☞ The court must listen to everything the accused and his or her lawyers have to say which is relevant to the defence.

☞ The accused has the right to remain silent at the trial.

☞ The accused has the right to make an unsworn statement, on which he or she cannot be cross-examined, from the dock.

☞ Once the court has reached its decision on whether to convict or to acquit, the defendant can never again be charged with that particular offence.

Members of the jury...

Who can serve on a jury?

Everyone between the ages of 18 and 65 who is on the electoral register, except
- those who work in the legal profession — judges, magistrates, lawyers, police, probation officers, prison officers, etc.
- members of religious orders
- the mentally ill — those who are resident in mental hospitals or who regularly visit a doctor because of mental illness, sub-normality or psychopathic disorder
- ex-prisoners — those who have been sentenced to five years or more in prison or who have been in prison for three months or more in the last ten years (People with convictions are not necessarily excluded.)

If you don't want to serve on a jury

The court has to allow you to be excused from jury service if you are a doctor, a dentist, a chemist, a nurse, a midwife, a vet, a member of the armed forces, an MP or a member of the House of Lords.
The court can allow you to be excused from jury service if it would be very inconvenient for you to serve — if you have difficulty in reading, or live very far from the court, or are solely responsible for a small business, or care for your children all day, or are ill, or for any other serious reason.

If you know the defendant or a witness

The clerk of the court should be told and you will be excused from jury service.

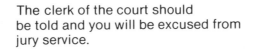

Your rights as a juror

- You have a right to choose a foreman (who may, of course, be a woman) from the jury. It does not have to be the first juror who is sworn in.

- You can wear ordinary, everyday clothes in court.

- If you feel ill or want to go to the lavatory during the proceedings, you should pass a note to the usher.

- If you fall ill and cannot continue as a juror, you will be excused. Up to three jurors may be excused without the trial being stopped.

- Each of you has a right to ask questions, through the judge, of any witness.

- As a jury, you can throw a case out at any time after the end of the prosecution evidence.

- You have the right to acquit even if the prosecution has proved its case. You can do this if you think the case should never have been brought, regardless of the judge's summing up.

- You should try to reach a unanimous verdict (one on which you all agree). Remember that every case before a jury carries a possible prison sentence.

- If you can't agree, the judge might instruct you that the court will accept a majority verdict of ten against two. If you still can't agree, the case might be retried or dropped.

- If there is any aspect of the case that you think should be brought to public attention, the jury foreman should read out a statement you have all prepared, after giving the verdict.

- If you object to comments made by the judge you can protest by stating your objections at the same time as your verdict.

Sentencing

There are three basic aims behind any kind of sentence:
• to punish — to make the offender suffer in proportion to the amount of harm he or she is thought to have done
• to deter — to frighten the offender from committing crimes again and to discourage other people, who may be thinking of committing offences
• to reform — to rehabilitate the offender, so that he or she no longer feels a need to commit crime

Judges and magistrates bear these things in mind when they are choosing an appropriate sentence for the case before them. Sentencing is very complex. Before a sentence is decided upon:
• a decision has to be made about just how severe the case is
• mitigating circumstances (particular reasons that might explain why a person acted in a certain way) have to be taken into account
• each individual's background and circumstances have to be weighed up

There is a maximum sentence laid down for most crimes but actual sentences vary, and it is the judge or the magistrate who makes the decision in individual cases.

Most sentences that can be given to adults can also be given to young people under seventeen, except imprisonment. If young offenders are sentenced to be held in custody, they are kept in borstals or detention centres.

These are the sentences that can currently be imposed on adults in England and Wales:

absolute discharge A person has been found guilty but is not punished. It usually indicates that the charge was not necessary.

conditional discharge If, within a period of up to three years, the defendant appears in court for another offence, then a sentence may be given for the original offence as well as for the second offence.

fine For most offences there is a maximum fine set by law. The defendant's means are taken into account when the fine is determined.

probation A probation officer supervises the defendant for between one and three years. This can only be done with the consent of the defendant.

community service order If a defendant has been convicted of an offence usually punishable by imprisonment, a court may order him or her to perform unpaid work in the community instead, like decorating or gardening, for any number of hours between 40 and 240. This too can only be made with the consent of the defendant.

imprisonment Most offences have a maximum period of imprisonment set by law. Prisoners are entitled to remission of one third off the sentence for good behaviour and are eligible for parole after one third of the sentence.

suspended sentence When a court passes a prison sentence of two years or less, it can order that the sentence shall not take effect. However, if between one and three years later, the convicted person commits another offence, the court can order the original sentence to take effect as well.

deferred sentence Courts have the power to defer a sentence for up to six months from the date of the conviction, to give the defendant time to 'turn over a new leaf', after which the sentence may be more lenient.

compensation order If the defendant has wronged someone, he or she may be ordered to pay compensation.

binding over If the defendant commits an offence within a certain stated amount of time after the court appearance, he or she must pay an agreed sum of money to the court. As well as convicted defendants, acquitted defendants and even witnesses have sometimes been bound over.

What sentence would you give?

Listed here are seven examples of criminal offences. In each case, the sentence that was actually given has been left out. Read the cases carefully and:

• decide which you think is the most severe case
• decide which sentence applies best to each case
• decide where there are mitigating circumstances and how they would affect your sentence
• decide what sentence you would give in each case

Now, compare your decision with the sentences that others in your group have given, and then compare these with the actual sentences.

If the sentences are different from your own, can you explain why?

1 A bus conductor was convicted of stealing 6p in fares from the local transport company, and of changing a bill in his favour.

It was his first offence, and he was described by the judge as previously being of exemplary character. He was given the opportunity to resign on two occasions rather than have the police brought in. But he said he was innocent, and stayed on at his job.

2 The 54 year old wife of a Lebanese banker was found guilty of stealing £2.05.

She had come to this country to see a doctor, as she was suffering from an illness. It was her first offence.

3 A young woman snatched a seven week old baby from its pram.

When she was fifteen she had a baby, which had been adopted. Later, when she was married, she tried unsuccessfully to start a family. She had pretended she was pregnant by putting towels underneath her clothes.

4 A 63 year old woman pleaded guilty to stealing a shoulder bag and two pairs of tights, valued at £16.35, from a London store.

Probation reports were read out in court. The defendant was a divorced mother of three children.

5 A sixteen year old boy from a depressed area was found guilty of attempted murder. With two other boys, he admitted asking a man for a cigarette and knocking him to the ground while his attention was diverted. The boys had taken five cigarettes from the man and a bunch of keys and 30p. The defendant had hit him with a brick as he lay on the ground, and the two others kicked him. The man was so severely beaten that doctors feared that his brain might be permanently damaged. The boy, who was said to be the ringleader, had never known his father. He had been in minor trouble before, and had been fined £10 the previous year for committing a disorderly act. Since leaving school he had been unemployed.

6 A young man was charged with four offences concerning an issue of a magazine. The issue contained a full page, reprinted from an American magazine, which gave instructions on how to make a Molotov cocktail and a hand grenade. He was convicted of inciting readers of the magazine to make explosives and to commit arson, but was acquitted of attempting to incite people to murder and to possess firearms to endanger life.

The judge asked for a report on his mental state, and said before passing sentence that nobody had been incited and that nobody took the defendant seriously. He had a previous conviction of two years for inciting people to riot.

7 A fourteen year old boy was found guilty of the manslaughter of a baby girl and the attempted murder of her sister, aged five.

The two girls were found by their mother in the bedroom of their council flat. The baby died from nineteen stab wounds and the sister had been stabbed eight times. The boy, who lived in the same block of flats, was said to be suffering from a personality disorder. A psychiatrist told the court that the boy was a dangerous person who did not have the control to stop himself from stabbing the children. He showed no evidence of insanity, but was withdrawn and aggressive.

These were the sentences given

1 He was sentenced to nine months' imprisonment. Eventually this sentence was quashed on appeal.

2 She was jailed for 30 days.

3 She was sentenced to two years' imprisonment, but was later freed on appeal.

4 She was ordered to do 100 hours' community work.

5 He was sentenced to 20 years' detention.

6 He was sentenced to do 200 hours' community work.

7 He was ordered to be detained for fourteen years.

Prisons

The most serious punishment that an adult in Britain can receive is a spell in prison. In March 1980 there were over 45,000 people in prison in Britain, more than at any other time this century. Here are some views about prison and its effects:

66 People value freedom, so taking it away makes them realise the seriousness of their actions. 99

66 The public needs protecting from people who would do them harm, so criminals must be shut away. 99

66 People are changed by being in prison: they have time to think about and regret what they've done. It gives them the opportunity to reform their ways. 99

66 Prisons don't actually put people off committing crime; out of every 100 prisoners entering prison in 1970, 45 had had one or more previous convictions. 99

66 Prisons today are very over-crowded. Home Office figures show that in our prisons 11,000 prisoners are sharing cells that were meant for one person only. 99

66 In my opinion, many of the people who are in prison don't need to be there. In a report on one prison in Birmingham, 23 per cent of 1064 inmates were serving sentences of six months or less, and 40 per cent of these were in gaol for failing to pay fines. 99

66 Imprisonment disrupts an offender's family, employment and housing and leaves a stigma long after the sentence has been served. 99

66 People in prison often make contacts with other criminals and get more deeply into the criminal underworld. 99

66 British prisons contain many people who could be better treated elsewhere — such as alcoholics, drug addicts, and people who are mentally ill. 99

Prisoners

Some prisoners have written vividly about their experiences.

Victor Serge

66 All men who have experienced prison know that its terrible grasp reaches out far beyond its physical walls. Prison marks one from the very first hour. . . it begins with the search, papers, letters, snapshots, everything that characterises the man, the little objects that accumulate around his private life — all this is taken from him. He feels as if he has been stripped of part of himself.

Nothing distinguishes one hour from the rest. Every man who is thrown into a cell immediately begins to live in the shadow of madness. Until the day of my release, I will be Number 6731: a prisoner, a robot programmed to obey prison rules. 99

Men in Prison. Victor Serge, Writers and Readers, London 1978.

Jimmy Boyle

66 The approved school surely played a vital part in my criminal development. It gave me connections that I was to find useful in my adult days . . .

The fact is that prison eats your insides out, and ties your stomach into knots, leaving your heart very heavy . . .

The solitary period was spent lying on the floor of the dark and very cold cell and this was interrupted for my one hour's exercise each day. 99

A Sense of Freedom. Jimmy Boyle, Pan Books, London 1977.

Jonathan Marshall

66 One of the first things you notice about a cell is the small Judas hole in the door, which allows somebody to look in but doesn't allow you to look out. As time goes by you learn to live with this spy-hole, which is like a hidden television camera, but you are never able to forget that it's there. It's amazing how ugly eyes can be.

Another thing you notice is that there is no handle on the inside of the door, and this is probably the most penetrating thing about a prison cell. It's a hard, cold fact that irrespective of what might happen in the cell — be it fire, flood, murder, illness or whatever — you, the prisoner, cannot open the door. 99

How to Survive in the Nick. Jonathan Marshall, Allison and Busby, London 1973.

Writers and Readers Publishing Cooperative

Caroline Tisdall

Valerie Wilmer

Prisons in Britain

This table shows the different types of prisons that exist for men and women in Britain.

Numbers in prison

The number of people in prison varies from day to day. This table shows the average daily population for the whole year, and gives you a chance to compare it with the number of places normally available.

Prisons for males	25
Closed training prisons	39
Open training prisons	9
Remand centres	11
Closed borstals (for young offenders)	14
Open borstals	10
Detention centres (senior)	12
Detention centres (junior)	7
Prisons for females	1
Closed prisons	3
Open prisons	4
Remand centres	3
Closed borstals (for young offenders)	2
Open borstals	1

Report on the work of the Prison Department 1980. London, HMSO.

Type of establishment	Normal accommodation (number of places) on 31 December 1980	Average daily population
Prisons for males	11 948	16 084
Closed training prisons for males	12 754	11 889
Open training prisons for males	3 502	3 190
Remand centres for men	1 836	2 265
Closed borstals for males	3 617	3 662
Open borstals for males	1 799	1 499
Senior detention centres for males	1 394	1 340
Junior detention centres for males	660	664
Grand total (male)	**37 510**	**40 593**
Prisons for females	552	682
Open prisons for females	483	422
Remand centres for females	177	227
Borstals for females	208	184
Grand total (female)	**1420**	**1515**
Grand total all establishments	**38 930**	**42 108**

Offences

This table shows the different types of crimes committed by women and by men. These are shown over four years, so you can compare the changes in the types of crimes most frequently committed.

Population of sentenced male prisoners by offence group, 1976-9

Offence group		1976	1977	1978	1979
Violence against the person		5956	6256	6202	6314
Rape		454	533	532	579
Other sexual offences		1154	1122	1078	1107
Burglary		10 183	10 414	10 708	10 253
Robbery		2140	2218	2160	2321
Theft, handling, fraud and forgery		11 149	10 298	10 120	9788
Other offences		3613	3434	3101	3287
Offences not known		629	472	697	932
All offences	Total	35 278	34 747	34 598	34 581

Population of sentenced female prisoners by offence group, 1976-9

Offence group		1976	1977	1978	1979
Violence against the person		160	160	195	195
Sexual offences		9	3	5	8
Burglary		126	123	107	116
Robbery		50	42	44	44
Theft, handling, fraud and forgery		452	519	504	542
Other offences		192	206	205	188
Offence not known		8	15	30	54
All offences	Total	997	1068	1090	1147

Lesley Nelson

There is increasing concern in Britain about the prison system: whether prisons are being used in the right way, and how to solve problems of overcrowding in prisons.

Read the views presented, and look carefully at the other information.

1 Do you think that prison is the answer for serious crime?

2 Do you think that prisons should be used more, or less?

3 Do you agree that certain offences should no longer be regarded as criminal, or that certain individuals should not be held in prison?

4 What differences do you notice between the figures given for offences committed by men, and those for offences committed by women? How might these differences be explained?

5 Can you or your group suggest alternatives to prison, and the kinds of crimes for which they might be suitable?

The structure of the courts

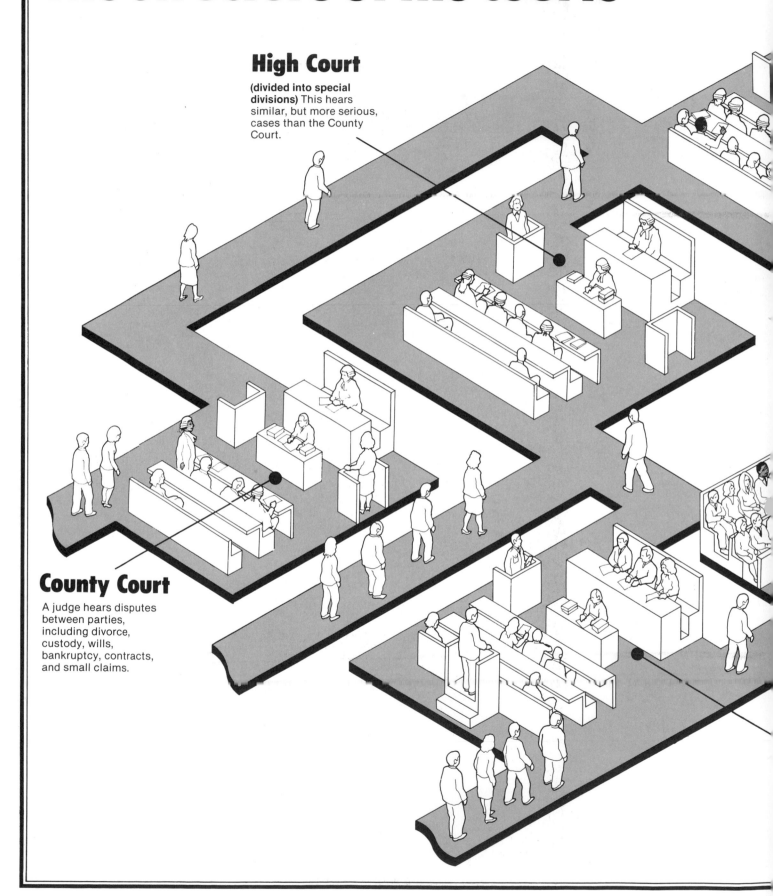

High Court

(divided into special divisions) This hears similar, but more serious, cases than the County Court.

County Court

A judge hears disputes between parties, including divorce, custody, wills, bankruptcy, contracts, and small claims.

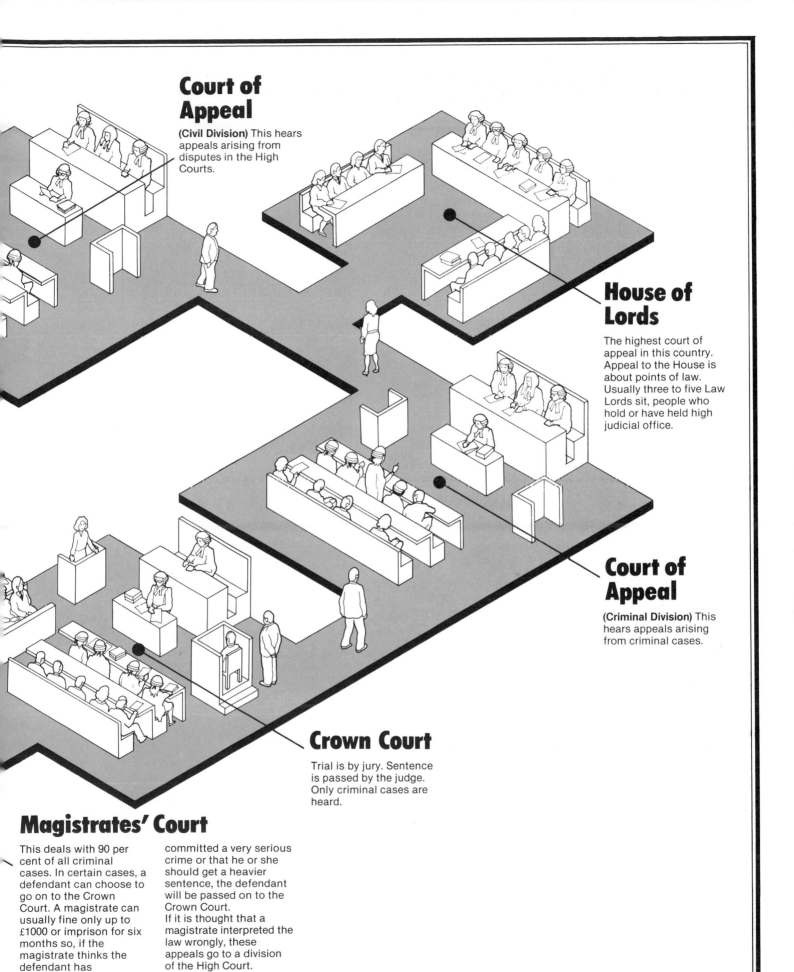

Court of Appeal

(Civil Division) This hears appeals arising from disputes in the High Courts.

House of Lords

The highest court of appeal in this country. Appeal to the House is about points of law. Usually three to five Law Lords sit, people who hold or have held high judicial office.

Court of Appeal

(Criminal Division) This hears appeals arising from criminal cases.

Crown Court

Trial is by jury. Sentence is passed by the judge. Only criminal cases are heard.

Magistrates' Court

This deals with 90 per cent of all criminal cases. In certain cases, a defendant can choose to go on to the Crown Court. A magistrate can usually fine only up to £1000 or imprison for six months so, if the magistrate thinks the defendant has committed a very serious crime or that he or she should get a heavier sentence, the defendant will be passed on to the Crown Court.
If it is thought that a magistrate interpreted the law wrongly, these appeals go to a division of the High Court.

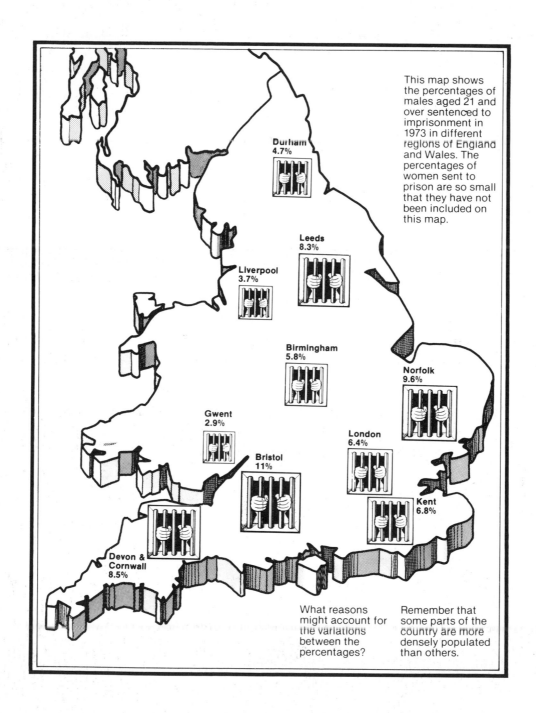

This map shows the percentages of males aged 21 and over sentenced to imprisonment in 1973 in different regions of England and Wales. The percentages of women sent to prison are so small that they have not been included on this map.

Durham
4.7%

Leeds
8.3%

Liverpool
3.7%

Birmingham
5.8%

Norfolk
9.6%

Gwent
2.9%

London
6.4%

Bristol
11%

Kent
6.8%

Devon &
Cornwall
8.5%

What reasons might account for the variations between the percentages?

Remember that some parts of the country are more densely populated than others.

Equal (almost) under the law

This chapter looks at the laws that have been passed in the UK to prevent discrimination on the grounds of race, sex and religion.

Discrimination means treating a person, or a group of people, less favourably than other people would be treated in similar circumstances, for no good reason. For example, if a woman who could not drive applied for a job as a bus driver, there would be good reason for not employing her. However, if she could drive but was refused employment for being female, that would be discrimination.

Groups of people who experience discrimination are often referred to as **minority groups**, even if they are not in a minority. For example women, who make up 51 per cent of the population of Britain, often experience discrimination and unequal treatment.

Stereotyping

When we are very young we start to find out that society expects males and females to behave differently. We are told that we must have certain attitudes and certain abilities according to our sex. This is called sexual stereotyping.

Even though each individual is unique, we are all expected to fit into the stereotype pattern of 'what girls are like' or 'what boys are like'. If someone says to you 'Don't be a tomboy,' or 'Stop being a cissy,' watch out — you're being stereotyped.

Many books used in schools reinforce a stereotyped view of male and female — like the example on the right.

In a book called *Science* in the Oxford Children's Reference Library series, 107 males are shown, and 17 females. The males are in a variety of active and scientific pursuits, while almost all the females are involved in domestic pursuits such as combing hair, vacuuming and mixing a pudding.

Another book called *Famous Writers*, published in 1970, mentions 34 men but not one woman.

In a recent study of the illustrations in 13 school chemistry textbooks published in the 1970s, the number of males and females shown was as follows:

Male	Female	Male and female together
258	26	16

Many advertisements also present a stereotyped picture of men and women — like the example on the right.

This boy is playing with a toy train.

This girl has a basket. She is going to the shop.

This girl likes to play with her doll.

This boy has a football. He is going to play.

If only a woman could get better looking every year

It isn't fair, but it's a fact: too many men get more attractive with the passing years. That distinguished greying at the temples...The look of maturity that comes with lines etched round the eyes and mouth...

With us, it's different. The merest hints of ageing skin must be taken care of as soon as they appear. Endocil beauty cream, used every night, will help to nourish and revive your skin. Light, non-greasy Endocil lotion, used each morning, will protect your skin right through the day.

Together, they'll help you keep its soft, supple beauty years longer. After all, why should men have everything their own way?

Endocil. All we promise is a lovelier skin.

Endocil

Butler Dennis Garland

68

At work, women and men in Britain still have very different job opportunities.

Women at work are found in a narrower range of jobs than men.

Women are usually found in catering, clerical, manufacturing or shop work, in nursing or teaching. Men have a much wider range of work open to them, and far greater opportunities for promotion.

Women earn less money than men.

The Equal Pay Act gives equal pay to women if they do the same, or broadly similar, work as men — so jobs like teacher, traffic warden and bank clerk are covered by the Act. However, because so many women do jobs which aren't done by men, and which are poorly paid, the average hourly rate of pay for women is only 73 per cent of the average hourly rate for men.

Women get fewer high status jobs than men.

Far more men than women hold senior positions in schools, for instance, although the majority of teachers are women. In 1978 in Sheffield, out of 2077 female primary teachers, only 111 were heads, while out of only 586 male primary school teachers, 116 were heads.

The picture on the left shows the proportions of women and men in certain professions.

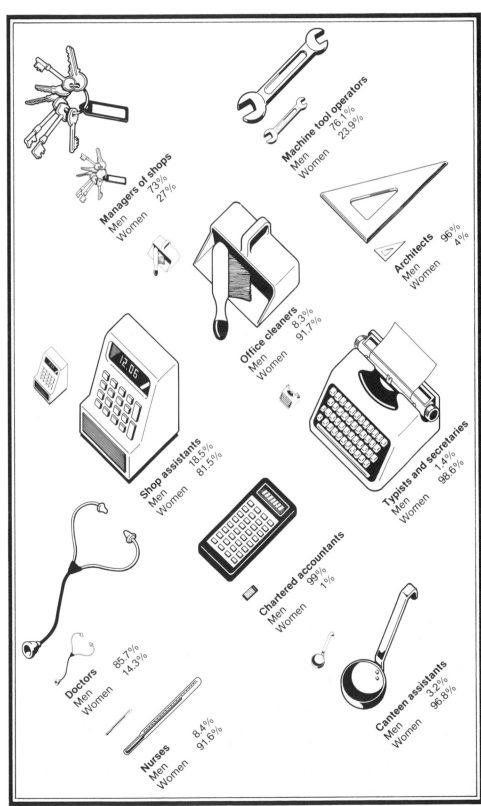

Machine tool operators
Men 76.1%
Women 23.9%

Managers of shops
Men 73%
Women 27%

Architects
Men 96%
Women 4%

Office cleaners
Men 8.3%
Women 91.7%

Typists and secretaries
Men 1.4%
Women 98.6%

Shop assistants
Men 18.5%
Women 81.5%

Chartered accountants
Men 99%
Women 1%

Doctors
Men 85.7%
Women 14.3%

Canteen assistants
Men 3.2%
Women 96.8%

Nurses
Men 8.4%
Women 91.6%

1 What expectations might be raised in the minds of girls and boys by the primary school reading book pictured on the opposite page? If you were preparing a reading book for young children, would you present the same kind of images? If not, what sort of images would you present, and why?

2 Write your comments on the Endocil advertisement, and discuss with your group the image of women presented in this sort of advertising.

3 Look at the advertisements on hoardings and in magazines, papers and comics for more examples of sexual stereotyping.
a) Describe what is happening in each one.
b) Write about each one, discussing the ways men and women are portrayed both individually and in relation to each other.
c) What effect could these advertisements have on the people who read them?

4 Look at the jobs in the picture.
a) Which of the jobs involve domestic work, for example, cooking, cleaning? Which sex usually does this type of work?
b) Which of the jobs involve supervising other people? Are these jobs held mainly by women or by men?
c) What changes would be necessary in schools and society so that different jobs could be done equally by both sexes?

5 List all the ways that you think boys suffer stereotyping just as much as girls:
• at home
• at school
• on TV, in films, books and magazines

6 Why do you think so few girls take exams in science subjects?

7 Do you think single-sex schools are a good idea? Give reasons for your answer.

8 What job do you want to do? If you were the opposite sex, do you think you would want to do something different? If so, why?

Towards equality in the law

During the late 1960s and the 1970s, new laws were made and existing laws changed to improve the position of women.

Some laws gave women a fairer share of property
It was recognised that where women stayed at home to look after a house and children, they were entitled to a share of the property after divorce (The Matrimonial Proceedings and Property Act 1970).

Some laws gave women equal rights in decisions regarding their children
Mothers and fathers were given equal guardianship rights over their children (The Guardianship of Minors Act 1971), and it was made easier for married women to obtain a divorce (The Domicile and Matrimonial Proceedings Act 1973).

Some laws gave women new protection from violence by men
It was made easier for women to obtain a court order preventing their partners from battering them (The Domestic Violence Act 1976).

Also in 1976, rape trials were made less of an ordeal for women: at these trials, the names of the people involved were to be kept secret, and the victim was no longer to be submitted to a gruelling and well-publicised examination of her private life (The Sexual Offences (Amendment) Act).

In 1978 another law came into force to protect women who have been attacked by their partners: the Court may now make an order to prevent the violent partner from remaining in the home (The Domestic Proceedings and Magistrates' Courts Act).

Some laws gave women improved employment and financial rights
A new pensions system enabled women to earn a good pension at work after having spent several years at home looking after their families (The Social Security Act 1975).

Some laws gave women rights they didn't have before
It was made easier for women to have legal abortions (The Abortion Act 1967).

There are two laws designed to prevent discrimination against people on the grounds of their sex: The Equal Pay Act 1970, and The Sex Discrimination Act 1975. Although these laws apply equally to both sexes, their main purpose is to improve the position of women, who have historically been at a disadvantage in employment, both in terms of job opportunities and pay. (You will find details of how The Equal Pay Act became law on pages 18 to 21.)

The Sex Discrimination Act 1975

Since 1975 it has been against the law to discriminate on grounds of sex in:
- employment and training
- education
- housing
- the provision of goods, facilities and services

So if a firm turns down a woman who is well-qualified for a job in favour of a man who is not so well-qualified, the firm may be acting unlawfully. This is **direct discrimination**.

If a firm requires all its employees to be over a certain height (which most women would not reach), the firm may be acting unlawfully. This is **indirect discrimination**.

However, there are many exemptions and exceptions to The Sex Discrimination Act. The Act does not apply in the following cases.

Work
- If you work, or apply to work, for a firm which employs fewer than six people
- If you attend a single-sex school or college

- If you belong to, or want to join, one of the Armed Forces
- If you work in a private household
- If you apply to work for a church (some churches will not ordain women)
- If you work all or most of the time outside Great Britain
- If you are male and want to work as a midwife (only a limited number are accepted)
- If you are female and want to work in a mine
- If there is a genuine need for someone of a particular sex to do the job (for example, an actor)

Housing
- If you try to rent accommodation in a house that the owner lives in or shares

Welfare services
- If you belong to a voluntary organisation or a charity whose main purpose is to provide benefits for one sex only (for example, Boys' Clubs)
- If you need special care, supervision or attention in a hospital, prison, hostel or old people's home

The Equal Pay Act 1970

Under The Equal Pay Act 1970, it is unlawful to pay a woman less than a man for doing the same or broadly similar work, or work that has been rated as of the same value as a man's, under a job evaluation scheme. If a shop pays its female assistants less than its male assistants for doing exactly the same job, or doing a very similar job, it is breaking the law. If it offers men promotion opportunities where they can earn more money, but does not offer these to women, it might be breaking both The Equal Pay Act and The Sex Discrimination Act.

These laws forbid discrimination against men as well as women.

The police don't have any power to operate these laws, however. The Equal Opportunities Commission can investigate and take action, but mostly individuals themselves have to complain to an industrial tribunal, or the Secretary of State for Education, or the county courts.

Since 1973 Britain has belonged to the European Economic Community (EEC). The EEC has the power to make laws, and has legislated equal pay for equal work. Some people, who have not been able to get equal pay under our Equal Pay Act, have gone to the European Court of Justice (which can make decisions which this country has to follow), and have been successful in their applications.

Equal treatment?
Jenny Smith

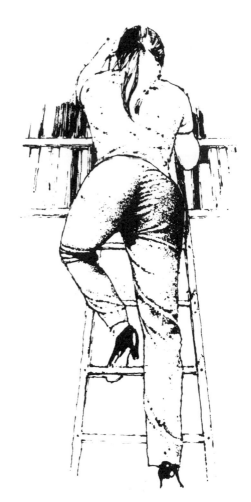

Jenny Smith was taken on to work in a bookshop for three months, to help with the incoming goods and with selling books. At her job interview the manager of the shop, Mr Hudson, told her that overalls would be provided.

For the first three weeks she worked in the goods department, where there was no contact with the general public. Then she was sent to work in the shop and she discovered that they had rules about the dress the staff wore there. Women who served in the shop had to wear blue overalls and were not allowed to wear trousers. There were no rules about what the men who served in the shop should wear, except that tee-shirts weren't allowed. They could wear any colour clothes they liked, and they didn't have to wear overalls. Jenny thought the trouser rule silly as she had to do a lot of bending and stretching, and climbing up ladders to reach high shelves. She thought it was unfair she had to wear overalls when the men didn't.

Eventually Jenny decided to ignore the trouser rule. She turned up at

work one day wearing her best navy blue trousers, thinking that they went well with her blue overalls. However, Mr Hudson told her that she must change into a skirt at lunchtime, and that if she continued to wear trousers she would get the sack. Jenny insisted on her right to wear trousers, and was told not to come back to work after lunch. She left the bookshop, and took legal advice. The people she asked agreed that it looked as though the only reason Jenny was not allowed to wear trousers at the shop was because she was female. This meant that she had a case under The Sex Discrimination Act. She discovered that because she and the other women had to wear overalls and the men didn't, she might have suffered a **detriment** (a disadvantage) under the Act. Jenny decided to take her case to an industrial tribunal.

Three months later, the tribunal heard Jenny's case. Jenny decided not to present it herself, but to let a friend present the case for her. The owner of the shop and the manager argued that the trousers rule was reasonable, and that all the other women in the shop accepted it. They claimed that the general public did not like to see women assistants in trousers. The overalls were useful, too, because customers could easily see who the shop assistants were.

They conceded that the men did not have to wear overalls, but felt that men only needed them for jobs where their clothes would otherwise get spoiled (like working in a butcher's shop), and that in this respect the women were at an advantage, as their clothes stayed cleaner under the overalls. Jenny, the manager and the owner left the room while the tribunal discussed the case.

When they were called back, the

chairperson told Jenny that they had considered her case carefully. He congratulated her on the careful way it had been presented. However, their decision was that she did not have a case: within the meaning of the Act, she had not been discriminated against. If there had been rules only for women and not for men, the tribunal ruled, that would have been discrimination. But men had to obey rules too — they were not allowed to wear tee-shirts. The tribunal feared that if they ruled in favour of Jenny's case, sooner or later a man would go to work wearing a skirt, and claim discrimination if he was told to change into trousers.

Although they agreed that she had been treated less favourably than the men in having to wear overalls, the tribunal unanimously agreed that Jenny had not been discriminated against. They felt that employers should have the right to say how they want their employees to look, especially when they are in contact with the public.

Despite this decision, Jenny was determined not to give up. She decided to go to the Equal Opportunities Commission (EOC). The EOC provided Jenny with a barrister to argue her case at an Employment Appeal Tribunal. The bookshop also employed a barrister, and at the tribunal several months later two barristers argued the case. Finally, however, the three members of the EAT ruled against her. The judge said that whilst he was sympathetic with her complaint, he could not, on this occasion, reverse the decision of the original tribunal. He felt that the fact that men did not have to wear overalls did amount to discrimination, but that Jenny's dismissal and her complaint both arose out of her refusal to wear a skirt, rather than on the question of overalls. Therefore he agreed with the decision already given.

Belinda Price

Belinda Price is a married woman with two children. When both her children were at school, she decided she would like to continue her career. She had done some office work when she was younger, and had enjoyed it.

In December 1975, Belinda answered an advertisement inviting men and women to apply for jobs in the Civil Service. However, she found that although she had the right qualifications, the Civil Service required all applicants to be aged between 17½ and 28. Belinda, at 34, was too old.

For the last ten years, Belinda had stayed at home to look after her children, and had been unable to take a full-time job. It seemed unfair that she should be prevented from applying for a job she wanted because of this. She felt that the age limit discriminated against women because, like her, many women in this age group stayed at home looking after young children. On the other hand, men weren't usually expected to stay at home and look

after children, and therefore they had an advantage over women. Belinda decided to complain to an industrial tribunal.

At the industrial tribunal hearing, Belinda argued that the age limit amounted to an act of discrimination under The Sex Discrimination Act. The Civil Service representative, however, pointed out that they had already raised the age limit from 23 to 28, and that equal opportunity did exist within the Civil Service. When the tribunal chairperson read out the verdict, Belinda was dismayed. 'Since it is physically possible for women between the ages of 17½ and 28 to apply for these jobs, these rules are not discriminatory.'

Belinda decided to appeal against the verdict. With the help of the National Council for Civil Liberties and the Equal Opportunities Commission, a case was prepared containing statistical evidence to back up Belinda's viewpoint. The Employment Appeals Tribunal decided that the case should be heard again before another industrial tribunal.

Eventually, two years after Belinda originally applied to the Civil Service for details of work, her case was heard again. This time, after hearing all the evidence, the industrial tribunal decided in Belinda's favour. They ordered the Civil Service to raise the age limit for applicants to 45 years. Belinda won her case, and the tribunal's decision will affect any woman (or man) who wants to work for the Civil Service in the future. It also means that any firm advertising with one age limit for women and another for men can be taken to court for unlawful discrimination. Belinda is surprised that no-one has used this precedent to bring cases against other employers who use similar age limits when recruiting staff.

1 For what reasons was Jenny's case dismissed?

2 Why wasn't Jenny allowed to wear trousers?

3 Do you think that employers should have the right to say what employees should and should not wear?

4 If you owned a bookshop, what advice would you give, or what rules would you make, about how your assistants should dress?

5 Discuss the following questions.
a) Why do you think Belinda Price brought her case?
b) Would she have won the case if she had been a man in a similar position? Give reasons for your views.
c) Was Belinda's claim one of direct or indirect discrimination?

6 The Sex Discrimination Act makes it generally unlawful for job advertisements to ask directly for a specific sex, except in certain circumstances (see page 71). Look through job advertisements in newspapers and magazines for those which are obviously angled towards one sex rather than another, even though they don't say so openly.

7 In order to make job opportunities truly equal, employers need to offer many different kinds of benefits. Make a list of benefits applying to both men and women.

Women and men in the law

This table shows the proportions of women and men involved in making and enforcing the law in England and Wales. Women are under-represented at every level, even in the lower status position of JP. A large number of women service the legal profession as secretaries, of course.

Practising barristers
Female 409
Male 4 003
Total 4 412
Source: Senate of Inns of Court and Bar

High Court Judges England & Wales
Female 3
Male 71
Total 74
Source: Lord Chancellor's Office

Circuit Judges England & Wales
Female 9
Male 300
Total 309
Source: Lord Chancellor's Office

Members of Parliament
Female 19
Male 615
Total 634
Source: House of Commons

Active J P s England & Wales
Female 9 543
Male 15 114
Total 24 657

Stipendiary Magistrates England & Wales
Female 2
Male 50
Total 52
Source: Magistrates' Association

Solicitors
Female 4 871
Male 41 710
Total 46 581
Source: Law Society

Police Force
Female 9 714
Male 105 828
Total 115 542
Source: Home Office

Total   Female 24 570   Male 167 691   Total 192 261

Percentage of women involved in the law = 15%

Is it against the law?

Look at the following examples, in which people have taken action on the grounds of sex discrimination, and at the decisions that were given in each case.

A woman was refused service in a coffee bar after 10.30 pm because she was alone. The manager said, 'Any females out alone after that hour must be prostitutes.'

Yes
The tribunal disagreed with the manager

A man applied for a job as a paper sorter and was turned down. He was told that the job was more suited to a woman 'because it was boring, repetitive work which a woman wouldn't mind doing'. He took the firm to a tribunal.

Yes
The firm paid him £100 compensation

A man was refused entry to a dance because his hair was too long, even though most of the women entering had longer hair than him.

No
The tribunal said that normal dress and appearance were different for women and men

A group of young people wanted to go swimming together but there were only single-sex pools in the area.

No
Neither sex was being treated less favourably

A shop assistant in a tailor's shop was dismissed because of her sex. The management said that the male customers might be embarrassed if she took their inside leg measurement.

No
The tribunal agreed with the management

1 At present, women in Britain can retire from work at 60, but men usually have to wait until they are 65. Yet women tend to live longer than men. Do you think that:
a) men should be able to retire earlier?
b) people should be able to choose their age of retirement?
c) the law should remain as it is?
Divide into groups and work out the points you would make in favour of a), b), and c), then have a debate.

2 Discuss the following questions.
a) What would you bear in mind if you had to decide whether the father or the mother should bring up the children after a divorce case?
b) Do you think that men should be able to stay at home while their partners go out to work?
c) Do you think that people who stay at home to look after children and to do the housework should be paid by the State for doing so?

3 Why do you think it was necessary to have a law on sex discrimination as well as a law on equal pay?

4 Look back at the exceptions and exemptions to The Sex Discrimination Act. Could any of these affect you? Are there any that you disagree with?

5 Look back over the examples listed in *Is it against the law*? Using your knowledge of The Sex Discrimination Act and your own experience, make up some cases for your group to discuss and to judge, as if they were members of a tribunal. (You will find more about industrial tribunals on pages 80-81.)

Gays and the law

**Homosexuality means sexual preference for people of the same sex.
Homosexual women are usually called lesbians.
'Gay' is the word that most homosexuals use to describe themselves.**

"When I began to realise that I was gay, I found it very difficult to accept, and for a long time I tried to pretend to myself that it was 'just a passing phase' or something that I could suppress.

Like thousands of other young gay women and men, I thought I was the only one. It was a lonely time and I was constantly afraid that somehow someone would find out.

When I finally told my closest friends (I was 19 at the time), it was because I could no longer stand the guilty feeling of deceit: I felt my friendships were based upon a lie. One or two people didn't understand at all, but on the whole it made little difference to my friends. It did, however, make a great difference to me. It was an enormous relief not to have to fear discovery and it was wonderful to know that I had friends who accepted me as I was. Not long after, one of them told me that he was gay as well, and that was magnificent. As more people came to know, I did get snide remarks and some ridicule but it was much easier to cope with because I had the support of friends to whom I had 'come out' (told I was gay). I found I quickly came to know more gay people, too, and their friendship was more exciting and valuable to me than any I had known.

Coming out isn't something that you do once and for all. Nearly everyone you meet assumes that you are heterosexual and attracted to people of the opposite sex, and you often have to make the decision whether or not to tell them you're gay. Sometimes I do and sometimes I don't, depending on the circumstances. It was years before I came out and told my parents about myself because I thought they would be too hurt and upset. When I did tell them they were shocked at first, but now our relationship is much closer than before and I can talk to them about what is really going on in my life.

Gay people still face discrimination and prejudice every day. Many people hide the fact that they are gay because they fear the reaction of families and friends, and are afraid they will become the victims of ridicule and abuse, or lose their jobs.

Once I took a job that I knew I wouldn't get if it was known that I was gay. I left after a while because I always felt insecure, fearing that I would be sacked if they found out.

Since those days, I've always tried to be open and honest about my sexuality. I prefer to argue with prejudiced people, rather than to feel guilty and insecure because I've hidden the fact that I'm gay.

There are gay women and men everywhere. We still face prejudice and we are still oppressed but we know now that we are not alone. We are standing together and fighting back. It can be exhil-arating. It can be fun."

Barry Prothero

Inner London Education Authority

Homosexuality is not uncommon: it has been estimated that in Britain one person in ten is homosexual, and many others have homosexual experiences or desires at some time during their lives.

For many years the law has discriminated against male homosexuals. Lesbians suffer from discrimination and prejudice too, even though the law does not usually interfere with them. It is not illegal for women to have homosexual relationships unless one of them is under 16 or is in the Armed Forces.

In England, Scotland and Wales all homosexual acts involving men under 21 are illegal. Since The Sexual Offences Act 1967, homosexual acts between males over the age of 21 and in private are legal.

In other countries the laws vary. In Sweden, the age of consent for gay men is 14. In Denmark, the age of consent is 15, in the Netherlands and Italy, 16, and in West Germany, 18. In Eire and Northern Ireland, homosexual activity is illegal between consenting males at any age. No laws have been passed anywhere which specifically legislate against lesbians.

One of the symbols used by those campaigning for gay people's rights is a pink triangle. This is the symbol that the Nazis forced homosexuals to wear in the concentration camps, where thousands of homosexuals were exterminated.

Jamie Dunbar

Jamie Dunbar worked as a porter in a big London hospital. Some porters were in the habit of wearing badges. He wore one saying, 'Yes, I'm homosexual too.' He was suspended from work and appeared before the Area Health Authority, represented by his trade union. He was given the choice of returning to work without the badge, or of losing his job.

This is part of the letter the hospital authority wrote to Jamie:
'I would like to make it quite clear that this hospital does not discriminate against homosexuals. Such matters are of no consideration in the employment of staff or their work in the hospital.

I explained to you that I felt that, by adopting a provocative attitude towards your homosexuality, you have invited incidents and conflict. The wearing of your badge, clearly indicating that you are a homosexual, is an example of this attitude and, by this, management believes you are taking up a campaign within the hospital. Incidents have arisen as a result of this campaign and I believe they will continue to do so as long as you adopt this provocative attitude. Such incidents are not in the best interests of the hospital.

Furthermore, I am of the opinion, having given serious consideration to the matter, that the badge you have been wearing may give offence to some patients and staff. I am sure you will appreciate that it is a sensitive time for patients when they are in hospital.'

Jamie chose to go on wearing the badge and was sacked.

YES, I'M HOMOSEXUAL TOO

Jenny Barnes

Jenny Barnes realised she was gay after eighteen years of marriage. She divorced her husband, who had treated her violently, and was granted custody of her two young children. Two years later, Jenny's ex-husband was remarried to a widow with four children. He told Jenny that he wanted the children back, and took her to court where he claimed that as a lesbian she could not be a good mother.

In court, Jenny was asked if she liked being the way she was. 'I told them I am what I am; it's not illegal to be a lesbian. My crime is being a lesbian mother.'

Jenny's partner, Susan, also appeared in court. In summing up, the judge said, 'I have no doubt that Mrs Barnes is a loving mother; the children are doing well at school and are well looked after . . . There is an undoubted bond between the mother and the girls.' However, he felt that 'her home lacks certain qualities, including the other partner, who is not the father figure . . . The court must do what is best for the children, and not necessarily what the children want.'

The judge heard the case for a day and then asked for four days' adjournment to consult other sources, as he confessed that he knew nothing about lesbianism.

Jenny lost custody of her children.

1 What is meant by the following phrases:
a) gay?
b) coming out?
c) heterosexual?

2 Look at the case of Jamie Dunbar and answer the following questions.
a) If you had to go to hospital, would you be offended or upset if you were wheeled in by a hospital porter wearing a gay rights badge?
b) If you had been in the same position as Jamie, would you have taken off your badge or would you have chosen to be sacked? Give reasons.

3 Look at the case of Jenny Barnes and answer the following questions.
a) On what grounds do you believe a court should separate a parent and young child?
b) Why did the court punish Jenny Barnes? Was the decision justified?

4 Why does society punish people for acts that are not against the law?

Racial discrimination and the law

The current law on racial discrimination, The Race Relations Act, was passed in 1976. Its intention is to prevent discrimination in employment, education, housing, and in the provision of goods, facilities and services, on the grounds of race or origin.

The law covers:

1 direct discrimination
that is, less favourable treatment on grounds of colour, race, nationality, or ethnic or national origins

2 indirect discrimination
that is, conditions which, although they apply equally to everybody, have an adverse effect on one or more racial minorities

The Race Relations Act also covers incitement to racial hatred: it is a criminal offence to use threatening, abusive or insulting language likely to stir up racial hatred, either in a speech in a public place, or in published material. The Act states that an intention to insult or discriminate isn't necessary: the action itself is enough.

One of the main changes made by the Act is that it gives individuals who have experienced racial discrimination at work the right to apply to bring a complaint before an industrial tribunal. However, under the Act, it is up to the individual to take the initiative and fight the case, and legal aid is not available for such cases. Tribunals are made up of representatives of management and the trade unions.

> The Race Relations Act doesn't apply in Northern Ireland. There, an earlier law aims to prevent both racial and religious discrimination: The Prevention of Hatred Act (Northern Ireland) 1970. This Act makes it an offence to use language in public, or to publish material, that is likely to stir up religious or racial hatred or fear.

A complaint brought under The Race Relations Act about discrimination at work must be registered on a form, called an IT1, within three months of the act of discrimination. Then the Advisory, Conciliation and Arbitration Service (ACAS) tries to settle the dispute without the need for a tribunal hearing. If a settlement can't be reached, the case must go before a tribunal. (Complaints about discrimination outside work are dealt with by the county courts.)

Racial discrimination at work

Outcome of industrial tribunal applications

	Withdrawn or settled	Dismissed	Successful
1977-78	80	61	5
1978-79	176	130	58
1979-80	223	181	22
Total	479	372	85

Mark Rusher

These people were discriminated against...

Mrs W, a white woman, was interviewed for the job of clerk/typist in 1977 by a director of a steelworks. He told her that the only other applicant had sounded West Indian on the phone and he had no intention of employing her as he 'did not have much time for coloured folk'. Mrs W then told him that she was married to a black West Indian. Later that day she was told that she had not got the job.

Mr P, an Indian, had over eleven years' experience in telecommunications when he applied for a job as a Technician Grade IIB. His application was refused after an interview in January 1978. At a tribunal hearing, the interviewers both said that they were concerned at Mr P's slight size and possible lack of resourcefulness, although this had not been discussed at the interview.

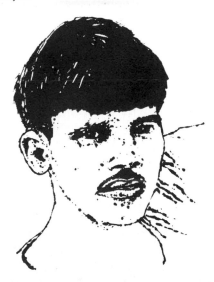

Mr K had over two years' heavy goods vehicle driving experience when he answered an advertisement for a driver with a haulage contractor. After discussing his qualifications and experience on the phone with one of the firm's directors, Mr K was asked for his name and address. When he replied 'Abdul K...' the director said, 'I don't think the lads would have that.' He added something about insufficient experience, and put the phone down.

Mr J, a Jamaican and a qualified wood machinist with eighteen years' experience, applied for a job at a timber firm. At the interview he clearly stated that he had four years' experience in metrication. Three weeks later, he was informed that the vacancy was filled. The job was readvertised twice, but whenever Mr J or a Jobcentre official contacted the firm, they were told either that the job required someone experienced in metrication (as Mr J was), or that it had been filled. However, a white friend of Mr J who applied for the job was later invited for an interview.

...and they proved it

A tribunal found that the steelworks had discriminated on racial grounds in not taking on a white applicant because her husband was black. The company was ordered to pay £75 compensation. This was the first successful case under the 1976 Act.

A tribunal decided that an act of unlawful racial discrimination had been committed against Mr P. He was paid £250 in compensation.

A tribunal decided that Mr K had been unlawfully discriminated against. He was awarded £50 for hurt feelings.

A tribunal found that Mr J was refused the job because of his colour, and awarded him £50 for injury to feelings.

1 'The law cannot change people's feelings.' Do you think this is always true?

2 Do you think that prosecutions under the Race Relations Act only serve to give extra publicity to the views of the prosecuted?

3 What ways can you think of to promote racial harmony?

4 Why do you think people are reluctant to bring a case of racial discrimination?

The case of

Farhath Malik was 18 and still at school when she applied for a part-time job in a chain store. Her parents were Pakistani and had brought her up in the Muslim religion.

In July 1979, Farhath was interviewed for a Saturday job by Ms Myers, the assistant staff manager at the Blackburn branch of the store. The interview went well until Ms Myers pointed out that she would have to wear the staff uniform of an overall over a skirt. Farhath replied that she wouldn't be able to wear such a uniform because her religion requires that women cover their legs. She felt she had no choice but to withdraw her application.

Farhath thought she had been discriminated against by the store. It was unclear to her whether she was being discriminated against on grounds of race or religion, and she knew The Race Relations Act 1976 didn't cover religious discrimination. Her parents, friends and teachers felt she was being discriminated against on racial grounds, and one of them wrote on her behalf to her MP. He sent the letter on to the Commission for Racial Equality (CRE) and Kuttan Menon, a legal officer, handled Farhath's case. (Not all cases are handled by the CRE: people can take cases to industrial tribunals on their own.)

The CRE staff helped Farhath to fill in all the details of her complaint on a long and complicated questionnaire. This would then be sent to the chain store, so that they could give their side of the story and return the form to the CRE. If the CRE thought there was a case to answer, they would ensure that another form (an IT1) would be sent off to start the tribunal proceedings. This all had to be done within three months of the incident.

The questionnaire was duly sent to

the chain store in September 1979 and, when they replied, the CRE weighed up the evidence and decided that it would finance the case. (If the CRE had not agreed to do so, Farhath would have had to pay for legal help, or would have had to represent herself throughout the case.)

Kuttan Menon warned Farhath that it was up to her to prove her case against the chain store, and not up to the chain store to disprove her accusations. She had to prove that she had suffered a detriment. Kutton Menon said that the tribunal had no power to order the chain store to employ her, but could only make recommendations. (If these recommendations were ignored, Farhath would have to take her case back to the tribunal or to a County Court.)

The CRE staff helped Farhath to fill in an IT1 form and begin the proceedings. The IT1 was first sent to the Central Office of Industrial Tribunals on her behalf. They sent copies to ACAS and to the store. The CRE failed to obtain undertakings from the store (through ACAS) to apologise to her, to pay her compensation, to agree that their action was unlawful and allow a tribunal to record this, and not to repeat similar actions in future.

Farhath Malik's case was finally heard in an ordinary room in an office building in Manchester, seven months after she had had her interview at the chain store, in front of three tribunal members — two men and one woman. Kuttan Menon, who was representing Farhath, had taken a lot of trouble to explain to her what the hearing would be like. Even so, she was nervous as she was called to give her evidence on oath. Kuttan had told the tribunal some of the background to the case, and he

80

Farhath Malik

started to question Farhath about the interview.

She found that once she had started to speak her confidence increased and she gave her evidence clearly and without hesitating. Farhath told the tribunal that she was given an application form and asked to fill it in. It contained the usual questions. She then went to the interview room with Ms Myers, who said:
'I am going to read it back to you so you can agree to it.'
Ms Myers asked her if she had any questions. Farhath's first question was:
'What would the job involve?'
Ms Myers gave her the details of her duties, pay per hour and tea breaks. Farhath then asked:
'Would I have to wear anything special, like uniform?'
Ms Myers told her about the regulation uniform and said:
'Are you asking all this because you're not allowed to wear a skirt? I thought you were just wearing trousers for the interview.'
Farhath replied:
'I'm sorry, I'll have to wear trousers. I won't be able to wear a skirt.'
She went on to explain why. Ms Myers then told her:
'For that reason you will be turned down and I won't be able to give you the job. Trousers are against the uniform regulations.'

Farhath's sixth form tutor gave evidence as to her character and the fact that she was well thought of by the staff of her school. Her tutor also pointed out:
'Farhath and other Pakistani girls are allowed to wear trousers as part of their school uniform; other girls are not.'

Kuttan Menon then called an expert witness, a lawyer called Doctor Pasha, to give evidence on the Muslim religion. He referred the tribunal members to the Koran. He told them that among other things it said:
'When a woman attains maturity no part of her body should remain uncovered except her face and the hand up to the wrist joint.' The Koran also forbids transparent clothing.

The chief personnel officer of the chain store argued in their defence that they required all female applicants for jobs in their stores to wear a skirt and an overall, and so they hadn't discriminated against Farhath. He said:
'It is easier for the general public to recognise a shop assistant when he or she is in a uniform and that uniform for women is a skirt and overall. Furthermore, we are a national chain store and our dress is the same all over the country.'

The tribunal retired to consider their verdict. Twenty minutes later they returned and the tribunal chairperson read out their verdict. He described Farhath as intelligent and personable, and said:
'It is perfectly clear that the Muslim religion does not allow women to have their legs uncovered . . . It is also a fact that in Blackburn there are some 14 per cent of the population who are . . . of Pakistani origin and of the Muslim faith.'
He continued:
'It is quite impossible for the applicant, or for that matter any Muslim woman, to comply with the store's regulation that they should wear skirts with trousers.'
In other words, if the regulation was upheld, no Muslim woman could gain employment in such a store. Therefore Farhath had suffered a detriment in the meaning of the Act because she could not comply with the regulation and so she could not take the job.

The chairperson continued:
'While the tribunal appreciate that the chain store's staff look neat and

tidy all over the country, other large stores in Blackburn allow Pakistani women employees to wear trousers under the skirt, and the trousers then become part of the uniform.'

The tribunal thought that any store in Blackburn would benefit if their Pakistani customers could see one of their race dressed in trousers under the uniform. They decided that it was a simple matter for the store to change their uniform regulations so that Farhath could wear a 'neat and tidy pair of slacks under her overall' if she wanted to apply to them for work again. They asked the chain store to change their regulation within 28 days.

Farhath was delighted with the result. She was glad that she had had the courage (and a lot of help from friends and the CRE) to bring her case successfully to a close. But during the time taken for the case to come to the tribunal, she had got a part-time job in a chemist's.

1 Using the information contained in the Farhath Malik story and in the preceding pages, could you explain the procedure for taking an employer to an industrial tribunal?

2 Do you have any suggestions for changing or improving the procedure?

3 Did you think the tribunal decision was fair? Give reasons for your answer.

4 Had Farhath experienced direct or indirect discrimination? Explain the reasons for your answer.

5 In 1973 a law was passed requiring motorcyclists to wear crash helmets. The purpose was to protect them from serious head injury in the event of an accident. In 1976 Sikh men, who traditionally, and for religious reasons, wear turbans, won the right to be exempted from this requirement. What are the arguments for and against making exceptions to the law for particular groups of people? In your view, are such exceptions justified?

Looking to the future

When times are hard for everyone, they're worse for black people. Some blacks believe in conforming, in doing well and getting on and, by integrating, improving the lot of black people in general; others believe they've been let down too often in the past, and reject white society to concentrate on their own culture. Even those who waver between those two extremes agree that many people in Britain hold racist views.

The attitudes of the militant, the disillusioned and the hopeful can be found in just one family unit. Nineteen-year-old Tony Poyser from Mosside, Manchester, is employed in a Jobs Project workshop run by the West Indian Sports and Social Club. Here he's found his first job since leaving school three years ago. Employment is guaranteed for only one year.

❝ Right now I don't think any black has any prospects. There's a whole heap of things they say about why they can't give you the job, like you haven't got enough qualifications, you've been out of a job too long — there's plenty. I think every interview I went to, I got a different excuse every time.

I thought differently when I left school. I thought that you could just leave school and get a job straight away. You don't. But we don't let those things get on top of us. If we let them get on top of us we would have cracked up ages ago. I can't even tell you how many times I've been picked up by the police; it's just been too many times. I get so sick of it now, it just doesn't bother me any more, I'm so used to it.

We've got to fight for what we want because we live in this country. I live in this country — I take it as my own — but for me to call myself an Englishman I've got to see everybody on equal terms with each other.

I love rebelling against people who try and put you down, just to show them that no matter what they do they can't put me down. I was born here but I don't class myself as British. We're part of it — but part of us remains separate from it. **❞**

Ira, Tony's younger brother, is studying for his A levels and, unlike his brother, has not yet turned his back on a future in British society. He wants to be a teacher.

❝ Sometimes I think my brothers are more right than I am. They are standing up for their colour, they're saying, "I'm black and this is what I look like," whereas if you look at me, I'm in Western clothes and speaking English and I'm just being brought up in a Western way.

Sometimes I wish I was like them: I like the hair and the clothes. I almost think it's a fashion, it came in and it'll go out like any other fashion. The depressive state will go because sooner or later black people will realise you can't go on fighting the system, you can't say , 'I hate all cops, I hate all teachers, I hate all social workers' because they are supposed to help and they don't. You have to say, 'Well, let's listen to them.'

I was suspended from school for fighting. I disagreed with it, obviously. For four or five years I'd been captain of this and captain of that and got top marks and then I was suspended, just like that. I hated everything. Then I thought about it and I realised I was responsible; it was me that was fighting.

It happened to me and sooner or later it'll happen to Tony to say, 'Well, we want jobs, we want to earn money, we want all the things that anyone else wants so therefore we've got to conform . . . **❞**

Preet Bains came to England from India when she was five. She now works as a supervisor at a women's centre in Southall, London.

66 When I was at school I was the only Indian child or one of, say, half a dozen. There wasn't so much of this racial hatred and we were treated quite decently.

When I got married I moved down to Hounslow. I was offered a job over the phone but when I arrived there and they found out I was an Indian they were reluctant to give me a job. The personnel officer thought I couldn't use a sewing machine properly. He'd got other Indians working there but he was treating them like slaves.

I don't think we'll get anywhere without fighting: we'll have to fight the people who bring in the prejudice, and the factory owners, even our own people if they want to exploit us. We will have to keep applying for jobs, re-applying for jobs and even going to the tribunals. That's the only way that it's going to be shown that this place is prejudiced and something will have to be done. 99

Harsev Bains is Preet's husband. He is the secretary of the Indian Youth Association of Great Britain.

66 Fifteen years ago, the problem for Asians here in Britain was language. People who came here were unable to carry out the jobs for which they were qualified, and there was hardly anyone running English language classes . . . My father himself faced this when he came here. In India, he was a headmaster. He's just retired as a bus conductor. That was all because of language, it wasn't so much because of colour.

But nowadays the problem is the areas where Asians live — areas where there were old, cheap houses where the whites no longer wish to live. Ghettos were formed there, because there was that type of work locally which the white man did not want to do. Now the industry is closing down. No money is being put back into the area by the companies. They have exploited the people — they have used them for cheap labour. Most Asians produce more work per person and are more loyal workers. They don't take it for granted the job is there for them. But now the young people are facing high unemployment.

When I was sixteen, I left everything, my parents included, to get a job. I came to London and joined London Transport. The department I went into, I was the first Asian. I did four years' apprenticeship with them.

Then I joined the place where I work now. I discovered quite a bit about racism at work. I'm an electrician by trade and I'm facing the abuse daily. When I'm working, some start coming and spitting on the floor around me and saying nasty things regarding my colour. If the management wish to harass me in any way, I cannot go to the shop steward because he also hates the colour of my skin. So there I am facing these two fronts. All I can do is try to mingle with the white workers there and ask them for support whenever I feel that I am being victimised.

I would like to think the future will mean a place where there are equal opportunities for black and white. But I don't think it will be here. In this system the best we can hope for is for the Government to implement the kind of statements that they say they are passing in our favour. It must start at Government level. Because if they continue on the same path that they have been going along for the past ten or fifteen years it might lead to a lot more troubles. We hope not. We hope that the Government has more sense because they're supposed to be learned people. Whether they are, only time will tell. 99

?

1 These interviews present a variety of attitudes and views. Compare the different approaches that these young people have taken to life in Britain for black people.

2 Which of the attitudes expressed above do you think is the most positive and useful for the next generation?

3 Why do societies tend to oppress minority groups?

Is equal enough?

Groups of people who have been treated unequally for many years often have difficulty in taking advantage of equal opportunities when they occur. For example, there are now more opportunities for women to work in senior management positions. The problem is that very few women have had the earlier opportunity to get the right kind of experience at a more junior level. So, although in theory they can apply for such jobs on equal terms with men, in practice men are more likely to be appointed because of their previous experience.

Some people think that equal opportunity isn't enough. They say that if women, blacks and other groups who have been discriminated against are ever to achieve equality with everyone else, they need to be given some extra help to do so. For example, employers could make sure that women as well as men get junior management experience by setting aside a proportion of jobs for them, and giving them lots of encouragement to apply.

This kind of action is called **positive discrimination;** it means giving one group some extra advantages in order to help them achieve equal opportunities. It's rather like the idea of handicapping in horse-racing.

Other people do not like this idea. They say that it's wrong to appoint people just because they're members of a disadvantaged group, and that any kind of discrimination is bad. They also argue that positive discrimination would lead to a lowering of standards; the best people for the jobs might no longer get them, and this would be bad for the country. Another point is that it would be difficult to work out over how long a period of time positive discrimination should take place. If it happened over too short a time, it would not really make much difference; if it happened for too long a period, other people would suffer from discrimination and loss of opportunity.

1 Explain the differences between equal opportunity and positive discrimination.

2 With which point of view do you agree?

Leaving school

Debbie's dilemma

'You never let me do anything I want!' Debbie shouted at her father. They were sitting over the remains of a Friday evening meal in the kitchen. 'I'm fourteen now,' Debbie continued. 'Donna is too and she has a job in a record shop every Saturday. I never have any money to spend!'
Debbie's mum came in from work and sat down at the table.
'You're not rowing again!' she said. 'What's up this time?'
'She's on about getting a job on a Saturday again,' said Mr Baker. 'Your teacher has said that you can't have permission because it will affect your exam results,' he added.
'I'm going to Donna's,' grumbled Debbie. 'You've no right to stop me getting a job. Neither has my teacher. I'm sick of you all!'

?

Can Debbie's teachers and parents stop her working? Is this fair? Does Debbie have the right to work?

1 Every family has its own rules, even if they are never actually spelt out. For example, somebody probably has first choice of TV programme; or there may be a set time when each child has to be home in the evening. See how many of your family's rules you can write down. Which of them do you think are unfair, and which do you argue about? Do you have more or less freedom than younger brothers and sisters? Were the family rules stricter when you were younger than they are now? Do the boys have more or less freedom than the girls? Who makes the rules in your family, and how are they arrived at? How many of these things are the same for other families in your group?

2 Do you agree with Debbie?
Can you put forward the arguments for and against Debbie's point of view?

3 Which of the following do you think should control the age at which young people can work?
a) the State
b) the school
c) parents
d) young people
Give reasons for your point of view.

Two years later...

Two years after the conversation with her parents about working on Saturdays, Debbie passed her exams.

In the end she was glad that she'd been stopped from working, although the extra money would have been nice.

Debbie was at school with two boys who lived in the same street as her — Frank and Steve.

The three of them still met occasionally, and compared notes as to how they were all getting along.

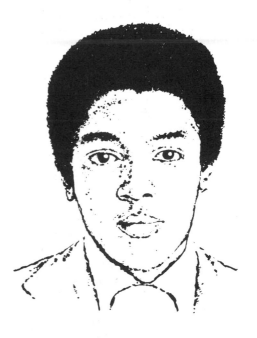

Frank worked on his father's stall in the market. He played truant from school to help out when his father needed it. Although he didn't pass any of his exams, he didn't seem to care. Debbie used to wonder where he got all his money. Frank was always able to pay for the three of them to go to the pictures.

Steve had always wanted to be a photographer. He decided to leave school as soon as he was sixteen, at the end of the Easter term. He had only passed three of his mock exams and had failed five, but he didn't think that would matter. His uncle Stan had told him that the best way to get started was to work in a photographer's, and learn the ropes.

How Steve survives

When they were at school, Frank had always said, 'It's OK in this country. If you don't get a job, you can always go on the dole.'
Steve had never trusted Frank's advice, and this time Frank proved wrong again. Steve wasted a day — and his bus fare — going to the unemployment benefit office. There he found that he couldn't claim unemployment benefit unless he'd already had a job. He needed to have paid at least 26 National Insurance contributions in any one tax year, and also to have paid most of the contributions due in the previous tax year. (The tax year runs from 6 April of one year to 5 April of the next year.)

When the interviewer at the unemployment office asked Steve for his **P45**, the tax form a worker is given by an employer on leaving a job, he had to explain that he had just left school, and had never even had a job. He was almost in tears as he explained that although he could go to the library each day to read the papers for job adverts, he needed money to phone for the jobs he saw, to post off applications, and for travelling expenses for interviews.

'It sounds to me as if you need to go to your careers office, my lad,' said the interviewer. 'You have to go there anyway before you can claim supplementary benefit.'
'What's that, exactly?' asked Steve. 'What do they teach you at school?' said the man. 'It's sometimes called social security, and you have the right to claim it. Since you're under nineteen and have just left full-time education, you're not eligible for supplementary benefit until the end of the vacation *after* your last term. Anyway, you have to go to your careers office first, before you come back to us.'

Steve was glad he'd left school at the end of the Easter term, as the holiday was only two weeks long. If he'd stayed at school for the summer term, he would not have been able to claim any money until the end of the long summer holiday.

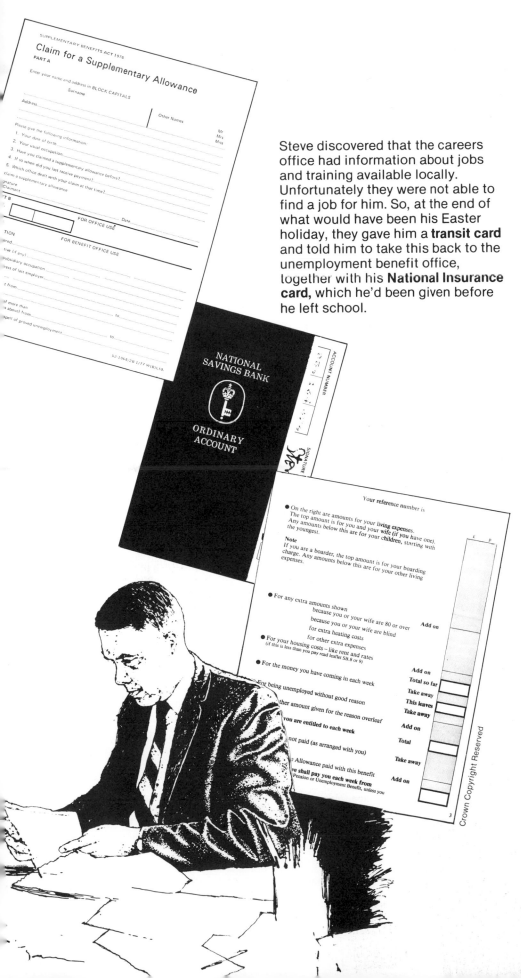

SUPPLEMENTARY BENEFITS ACT 1976

Claim for a Supplementary Allowance
PART A

Enter your name and address in BLOCK CAPITALS

Surname

Address..

Other Names

Mr
Mrs
Miss

Please give the following information:
1. Your date of birth.........................
2. Your usual occupation.........................
3. Have you claimed a supplementary allowance before?.........................
4. If so when did you last receive payment?.........................
5. Which office dealt with your claim at that time?.........................
claim a supplementary allowance

nature
Claimant

T 8

FOR OFFICE USE   Date............

TION   FOR BENEFIT OFFICE USE
ered..........................
tive (if any).........................
subsidiary occupation.........................
ress of last employer.........................
t from.........................
of more than
s above from.........................to............
pell of proved unemployment.........................to............

52-1068/2B 1/77 W(B)Ltd.

NATIONAL SAVINGS BANK

ORDINARY ACCOUNT

ACCOUNT NUMBER

SIGNATURE

Your reference number is

• On the right are amounts for your **living expenses.**
The top amount is for you and your **wife (if you have one).**
Any amounts below this are for your **children,** starting with the youngest.

Note
If you are a boarder, the top amount is for your boarding charge. Any amounts below this are for your other living expenses.

£   p

• For any extra amounts shown
because you or your wife are 80 or over
because you or your wife are blind
for extra heating costs
for other extra expenses   **Add on**
• For your housing costs – like rent and rates
(if this is less than you pay read leaflet SB.8 or 9)

• For the money you have coming in each week   **Add on**
          Total so far
 For being unemployed without good reason   **Take away**
ther amount given for the reason overleaf   **This leaves**
          Take away
you are entitled to each week   **Add on**
          Total
not paid (as arranged with you)   **Take away**
Allowance paid with this benefit
ve **shall pay you each week from**   **Add on**
Pension or Unemployment Benefit, unless you

3

Crown Copyright Reserved

Steve discovered that the careers office had information about jobs and training available locally. Unfortunately they were not able to find a job for him. So, at the end of what would have been his Easter holiday, they gave him a **transit card** and told him to take this back to the unemployment benefit office, together with his **National Insurance card,** which he'd been given before he left school.

When Steve arrived back at the office, he was given **Form B1** to fill in. The officer then made an appointment for him at his nearest Department of Health and Social Security (DHSS) office, and told him to take his Form B1, his rent book (if he lived away from home) and a savings book if he had one. At this appointment, Steve was asked where he lived, what rent he paid, and whether he had any savings — but they still didn't give him any money.

The following week, a woman called at Steve's house. She was from the DHSS, and Steve realised that she was checking whether he had given true details about himself.

Later that week he got a Giro money order through the post. His mother told him to take it to the post office, where he was able to exchange it for cash. After that, a money order came through every fortnight while Steve was unemployed.

Steve also discovered that he had a right to ask for a **notice of assessment** if, for instance, he thought he was not getting enough money. This would show how the DHSS office had worked out his claim.

Steve finds a solution

Steve visited his careers office regularly and they told him to go to his local Jobcentre (or employment office) too. At the Jobcentre, there were cards on display boards offering work under different headings.

Along with other job hunters, Steve looked through the cards, and made a note of the reference numbers at the bottom of any cards offering work that seemed suitable. He found that the receptionist would arrange interviews for these jobs, and that he didn't have to fill in any application forms for them.

Steve had five interviews arranged in this way, but he didn't get any of the jobs. After the last unsuccessful interview, he complained to his parents, 'I can't get a job because I haven't got experience, and I can't get experience because I haven't got a job!'

He repeated this to his careers officer the next day. She nodded sympathetically and suggested that Steve should try one of the Government schemes specially set up to help unemployed young people to prepare for work and to improve their chances of getting and keeping jobs. She explained that nowadays unemployment was a problem for everyone, not just young people.

Steve could apply to do one of the Youth Opportunities Programme (YOP) schemes open to all young people between the ages of sixteen and nineteen who had been unemployed for six weeks or more. These schemes include both work preparation courses and work experience schemes.

Steve decided he would apply for a work experience scheme on an employer's premises. His careers officer agreed that this was probably the right choice for him. She reminded him that it wouldn't be a permanent job and that he should go on applying for other work while getting the experience, as work experience was guaranteed for only a year. After that he would have to register as unemployed again. But as Steve said, 'At least I'll be doing something.'

1 Steve was probably misinformed by Frank and by his uncle Stan; if he'd had better advice maybe he would have been a bit more realistic about what he wanted to do and how to go about things.
What kind of help do you think people like Steve need to get at school, and how do you think this should be organised?

2 Some trade unions have stated that they object to schemes like the Youth Opportunities Programme. They think that they are both bad for the individuals involved and also for other workers in an industry. What reasons could they have for taking this point of view? What do you think?

3 Find out about your local Youth Opportunities Programmes and work experience schemes. Perhaps some of the pupils in your college or school are already doing work experience; if so, interview them about their feelings towards it.

4 Make up a poster or leaflet for young school leavers explaining what they should do if they leave school and can't get a job. It should be simple and clearly laid out. You'll probably need to look back through Steve's experiences in order to establish clearly the different stages that he had to go through and the opportunities that he was offered.

5 Using your local telephone directory, write down the addresses and telephone numbers of the following:
a) your local careers office
b) your local unemployment benefit office
c) your local Department of Health and Social Security office

Work preparation courses help young people to decide what kind of work they would like to do, and give them training in a variety of skills. There are three types of courses:
a) short training courses, which last for about twelve weeks and teach some of the basic skills needed in the local industries
b) work introduction courses, which last for about thirteen weeks and are intended for young people who haven't got on too well at school
c) employment induction courses, which last for only two weeks, but give young people a chance to try different skills.

Work experience schemes all include training, education and advice. Steve could stay on one of these for up to twelve months. He could leave immediately if he found a job, and would be allowed time off to look for work. Whilst on the programme he would receive a weekly allowance slightly higher than supplementary benefit. The schemes include:
a) work experience on an employer's premises, which could be in industry or in an office
b) project-based work experience, which would involve Steve in working with other young people under supervision on a new community project
c) training workshops, in which Steve would gain skills while working to produce goods
d) community service, consisting of projects in places like adventure playgrounds, luncheon clubs for the elderly, or hospitals

The truth about Frank

'What are you smiling about?' asked Frank, bumping into Steve in the street.

Steve told him about his application to do a Youth Opportunities Programme scheme and how it would mean that he'd have a bit more money than he'd been getting on supplementary benefit. Frank laughed.

'You could be getting big money like me.'

'Oh yeah, how? We haven't all got dads who can give us a job on the market,' Steve retorted.

'That's just peanuts compared to what I can pick up on the side,' said Frank. 'Pick up a motor, take it for a spin and see what you can lift from inside. Get it?'

Steve got it and decided he wanted to forget it. He was glad he had, because next day Frank was picked up in a stolen car by the police. He had the owner's wallet in his pocket, and two car radios in his bag.

Frank was taken to the police station where he was asked his age. When the police discovered he was sixteen, they put him in a room by himself while they tried to contact his parents. This was because, as a juvenile (under seventeen), he had to be questioned in the presence of his parents or another adult (other than a police officer).

Frank didn't know which he was dreading more — his father's arrival or the questions he was going to have to answer. When they arrived, his father was furious, his mother ashamed and crying.

The questioning didn't take long and Frank was charged with 'taking and driving away' and theft. He was worried that he would be detained on remand until his case was heard in court. He asked the police officer what his chances were of getting bail, and was told that he would be given bail unless the police felt that:
a) he wouldn't attend court
b) he would commit more offences while on bail
c) he would interfere with the police case against him
d) it was in his own interests to be held in custody
e) the crime he had committed was very serious, like murder

Frank was relieved to be released on bail, after his parents had signed a surety for £200. His father pointed out that he would have to pay that amount to the court if Frank didn't turn up for his trial.

'Tomorrow you're going to look up the number of the local law centre in the phone book and ask them to recommend a solicitor, my lad,' his father said. Frank made an appointment for himself and his mother and father to see a solicitor, called Joan Hunt, later that week.

Although Frank didn't earn much and had no savings, he wasn't entitled to legal aid because he was living at home and was employed by his father. His parents' income was also taken into account. His father told him he'd have to pay back the money his parents had spent on solicitors' bills.

Frank was relieved to find that the solicitor took the trouble to explain the law to him and his parents. 'If you had been caught committing a crime with a person who was over seventeen, you would have had to appear in a Crown Court, but since you were on your own, the Juvenile Court will deal with this.'

The solicitor asked Frank whether or not he was guilty, and Frank admitted that he was. She told him that he would have to plead guilty but that she would appear in court for him.
'Is there anyone who can testify as to your character?' she asked.

Frank thought about asking one of his old teachers, but decided not to when he remembered the amount of trouble he'd been in at school. With a sinking feeling, he realised he had no one to put in a good word for him. He told his solicitor, and she said that that was what she was there for. She talked to him and his father for another half an hour, asking details about the family.

Some weeks later, Frank got a letter telling him when his case would come before the court. It seemed to him that he would have to wait for ever.

On the morning of his court appearance, Frank arrived at the Juvenile Court with his parents, feeling stiffly uncomfortable in a new shirt and a suit he hated. His terror was partly because he didn't know what to expect, and partly because he knew he was guilty.

He asked Joan Hunt whether his name would be in the papers. She reassured him. 'The public are not allowed to attend a Juvenile Court. Only the magistrates and court officers, people involved in the case, and newspaper reporters are allowed to be present. But those reporters aren't allowed to print your name, or your address or anything which would tell people who you are.'

At that she left Frank, and went into the courtroom. After a while Frank's

name was called out and he and his parents went in. They were shown to some seats right at the front. Immediately before them were three magistrates, sitting at the same level as Frank. To his right sat his solicitor with the clerk of the court and other solicitors. On his left there was a witness box, and sitting next to it was the person who had called out Frank's name, the usher.

One of the magistrates explained to Frank what the charges were, and asked him whether or not he admitted the offences. Frank said in a very small voice that he was guilty. The magistrate then told the usher to call the arresting officer. As the police officer walked into the court and took his place in the witness box, Frank recognised him as one of the officers who had found him with the car and the stolen goods.

After taking a Bible in his hand and swearing to tell the truth, the police officer briefly explained what Frank had done, and how he'd been caught red-handed. He drew the court's attention to the fact that Frank had two different car radios in his bag.

When he had finished, the magistrate asked Frank and his parents if they were represented. They nodded. It was the first time Frank had seen his father at a loss for words.

Debbie discovers her rights at work

In her last term at school, Debbie had started to apply for jobs. Her school results and estimated grades were good and she was conditionally accepted as a trainee technician by a local firm that made parts for computers.

One of Debbie's teachers at school, Mr Foster, had arranged for Mrs Patel from the local Citizens' Advice Bureau to come and talk to all the school leavers about their rights at work.

The contract of employment

Mrs Patel started her talk by telling them about agreements with employers:

'When someone offers you a job and you accept, there is a contract between you. This is a legal agreement between an employer and an employee which defines the rights and responsibilities of both parties towards each other. The contract states: what your job is and what it involves; when it began; your pay; your hours of work; your holidays; the length of notice needed by either side; how you should deal with problems in the workplace; and what happens to you if you are sick or get the sack.

It won't always be written down in one place. You may find out about it in the job description that you saw in the Jobcentre or that they sent you with the application form, or in the letter you had offering you the job, or in a written statement. It also depends on the way people have got used to working in your firm — which is called the "custom and practice" of the workplace.'

Debbie asked Mrs Patel what the responsibilities of the employees were. Mrs Patel replied:
'You have duties towards your employer. These are: to carry out all reasonable orders so long as they are lawful; not to commit misconduct; to give faithful and honest service; and to use reasonable skill and care in work.'

 'It sounds just like school,' muttered one of Debbie's friends under his breath. 'Not quite,' said Mrs Patel, who had good hearing. 'You don't get paid at school.'
Everybody laughed, and she continued: 'An employer has duties towards his or her workers. These are: to take reasonable care for the workers' safety; to pay the agreed wages; not to require the employee to act unlawfully; and to provide work, if available, for employees who are paid by commission or according to their results.'

The hours

 'What about the hours you work?' asked Sue, one of Debbie's classmates, notorious for not being able to get up in the morning. Mrs Patel answered: 'The hours you work are usually agreed between the employer and the union or workforce. You'll be told how long shifts are and what breaks you get. There are certain laws restricting the hours you can spend doing manual work in a factory, for instance, which apply to women and people under the age of eighteen.'

Debbie pricked up her ears. She would be working on the shop floor of the factory as part of her training. She asked Mrs Patel what these laws covered.

Mrs Patel explained:
'Although there are some exceptions, as a general rule, you shouldn't work more than nine hours a day, or 45 hours a week (without overtime). You must not work more than nine hours continuously without a half-hour rest break and you mustn't start work before 7am or end after 8pm.'

 'It's worse than the sixth form,' said Sue in disbelief. 'What about the holidays — are they any better?'

The holidays

Mrs Patel answered: 'The amount of paid holiday, if any, depends on what your contract of employment says. You don't *automatically* have a right to a paid holiday, even to a paid bank holiday, though most employers pay these.'
She continued:
'Your employer must pay you in cash, or by cheque, or straight into the bank. You must be given a **pay slip** with your wages. This sets out how much you earn before tax, what is deducted and taken from your wages — income tax, National Insurance contributions, and so on.'

The deductions

 'Why is money taken from your wages?' asked Debbie. Mrs Patel explained: 'National Insurance goes towards National Health treatment, which includes doctors' and dentists' salaries and so on. If we didn't have this, you'd have to pay for all those things separately, as they do in many countries, and this can be very expensive. National Insurance also pays for pensions when you retire, and sickness and unemployment benefit.

Tax is also taken off before you get your pay. This system is called PAYE — "Pay As You Earn". Your tax goes towards the cost of hospitals, schools, etc. It also contributes towards the incomes of the State and of the armed forces, and to the cost of building and upkeep of roads and railways.'

Time off for sickness

 'What happens if you're off sick?' asked Debbie. Mrs Patel replied:
'As with holidays, there is no law saying your employer has to pay you while you're off sick. But most employers (about 70 per cent) are covered by some kind of sick pay scheme. Again, you must ask your employer or your union. If you're sick, or if you can't work because of serious injury, you should be entitled to social security payments. Your employer may require you to produce a medical certificate if you're off work for longer than three days, but you will *need* a certificate from your doctor to claim sickness benefit from the social security office.'

 'But what happens if you have to take time off to go to the doctor?' asked Sue, who suffered badly from hay fever.

Mrs Patel explained:
'Taking time off is up to the employer, who doesn't have to pay you for it, unless your contract provides for paid leave.'
She concluded: 'Remember, all the things I've told you are only general points; when you start work you'll probably want more detailed information. Never be afraid to come to the Citizens' Advice Bureau to ask our advice. That's what we're there for.'

1 In what ways are your rights and duties at work different from your rights and duties at school?

2 Do you think that your wages should be automatically taxed? What services would you rather pay for yourself, if you had the choice? Write down your reasons.

3 It has been suggested that taxes paid by young people between sixteen and eighteen should be spent only on projects specially aimed at this age group. Do you think this is a good idea? How would you suggest the money should be spent?

4 Discuss with your teacher how to set up an 'advice bureau' for new pupils or students to help answer their questions. Could you prepare a booklet giving basic information about school or college, based on your own memories of questions that you had in your first weeks? Perhaps you could even set up a bureau yourselves to answer questions for new arrivals at your school or college.

5 Make a list of the questions that you would like to have answered by an expert like Mrs Patel. You could then find out about your own local Citizens' Advice Bureau, gather your group's questions together and (with your headteacher's permission) contact the experts at the Bureau for advice.

Debbie decides about trade unions

On her way home from school, Debbie met Steve and Frank and invited them in for a cup of tea. Her parents came in as she was telling them about the trade union official who was due to come to the school on the following day.

'Oh, yes,' said her mother, 'when you start work you'll have to join the union.'

'Not if you don't want to,' said her father. 'Anyway, all they want from you is your money — you don't get anything back. Layabouts, that's all they are. If you join, you'll be on strike the first week you start work. And then where will you be? Out of work — that's where.'

Debbie's mother retaliated: 'Employers don't give you wage increases out of the goodness of their hearts, you know — they only give them because of pressure, and trade unions are organised pressure. And as for all those people who don't want to join a union — have you ever heard of them refusing better pay or working conditions when the union has negotiated them? I saw a programme on the telly last week which showed that more working days are lost in Britain through illness than through strikes.'

Debbie sighed. She'd heard this argument before but had never been in a position where she had to decide for herself. So she worked out some questions to ask the trade union official.

The background

Mr Foster introduced Mr Pollard to the class the next day by telling them that he wasn't there to recruit people for his union, but just to tell them about trade unionism in general and answer their questions.

Mr Pollard began:
'When you're working, and you want better pay, better holidays or better conditions at work, you'll find you won't get very far on your own. Anyway, it's better for everyone to ask for the things they want, together. And remember, problems at work aren't just about pay and holidays. It's important to work in decent surroundings and to know that the machines and materials you work with are safe. You also need to know that the work is shared out fairly and that you're doing the job you want to do.

Even when your rights at work are protected by law, in practice they may only be achieved through union representation. People not in a union are in a much weaker position when it comes to obtaining those legal rights. The union normally succeeds in negotiating much more favourable conditions than the law provides.

All major unions come together in the twelve-million-strong Trades Union Congress — the TUC. If you don't know which union to join when you start work, write to the TUC.'

Closed shops

Debbie decided to ask her first question:
'Do you have to join a union, and what's a closed shop?'
Mr Pollard replied:
'If you get a job in a place with a closed shop, you have to join the union when you start work, otherwise you'd be sacked. But if the employer dismisses you for refusing to join a closed shop for religious reasons or some other deeply held personal conviction, or if you began work before the closed shop agreement came into force, it's unfair dismissal, and you should be able to get compensation.'

Union meetings

'Union meetings are often held in the same room where you work. You and your workmates gather to talk about any problems you are experiencing. Together you're known as a *shop.* Each shop has an unpaid representative elected by them and answerable to them — the *shop steward.* Each union member automatically belongs to a branch, a subdivision of the union which covers several firms close by, and has a meeting every month after work. It's important to attend branch meetings to find out what the union is doing, and to express your views and help decide union policy.

All unions have regular conferences, usually every year, where they decide on new policies. You elect members from the branch to go to the conference as delegates, and the branch decides whether to vote for or against various policies.'

Tim, one of the boys in the class, said:
'My dad says all the money you pay the unions goes to the Labour Party. Well, I don't agree with that. I'm going to vote Liberal when I'm eighteen.'
Mr Pollard laughed.
'If the trade union you join is affiliated to the Labour Party,' he said, 'a small part of your subscription goes as a contribution to Labour Party funds. You can opt out of this, though, by taking advantage of the conscience clause. It just involves signing a standard form.'

Going on strike

Another boy, Brian, said:
'My dad says that all unions do is go on strike.'
Mr Pollard replied:
'Most trade unionists never go on strike. Sometimes you have to, and it's usually because your employer refused to listen to your arguments in negotiations. But people don't go on strike lightly. You're not paid while you're on strike. You may get strike pay from your union and, if you have dependants, they may be entitled to state benefits, but they're a lot less than your usual pay.'

Debbie had a sudden thought. 'Can you be sacked for going on strike?' she asked.
Mr Pollard looked serious and said:
'Well, it is lawful for an employer to sack you because you go on strike. However, this happens very rarely.

All of you should remember that unions are only as effective as the people in them. If and when you join, make sure you go to all the meetings and play your part in getting what we in the unions call "a better quality of working life" for everyone.'

---

1 Can an employer dismiss you for:
a) belonging to a union?
b) taking the afternoon off to go to a union meeting?
c) striking?

2 The following list shows some of the things a union should provide. Arrange them in order of importance.
A union should:
● give you more power to ask for what you want
● help you win better pay
● protect you if you're sacked unfairly
● help you if you're made redundant
● make sure you have the right training
● help you get better holidays
● fight for you if you face discrimination because of your race, colour, or sex
● help you get safer working conditions
● help you fight for a better working life
Add anything else to the list that you think a union should do for its members.

3 Find out what the following abbreviations stand for: TUC, TGWU, NUT, AUEW, NUPE.

4 Has your school or college got a students' council? In what ways is your council the same as, or different from, a trade union?

5 Select two different types of daily newspaper and gather together all the articles, features, and comments that they have printed on the subject of trade unions over a period of, say, three weeks.
a) Can you make any observations about the way that the two newspapers present the subject?
b) What sort of 'image' of trade unions do your papers present?
c) Is there much more material in one paper than the other?
d) Is there a difference in the types of headlines that the two papers use?
e) Is there a difference in the style in which the items are reported?
Discuss the differences and the similarities that you have noticed between your papers and those of others in your group.

Whose right at work?

The laws that govern people's rights and responsibilities at work are many and varied. People very often have difficulties finding out what their rights are. The letters on this page are typical of problems that people at work often have to sort out. Read them carefully and then study the box on the right.

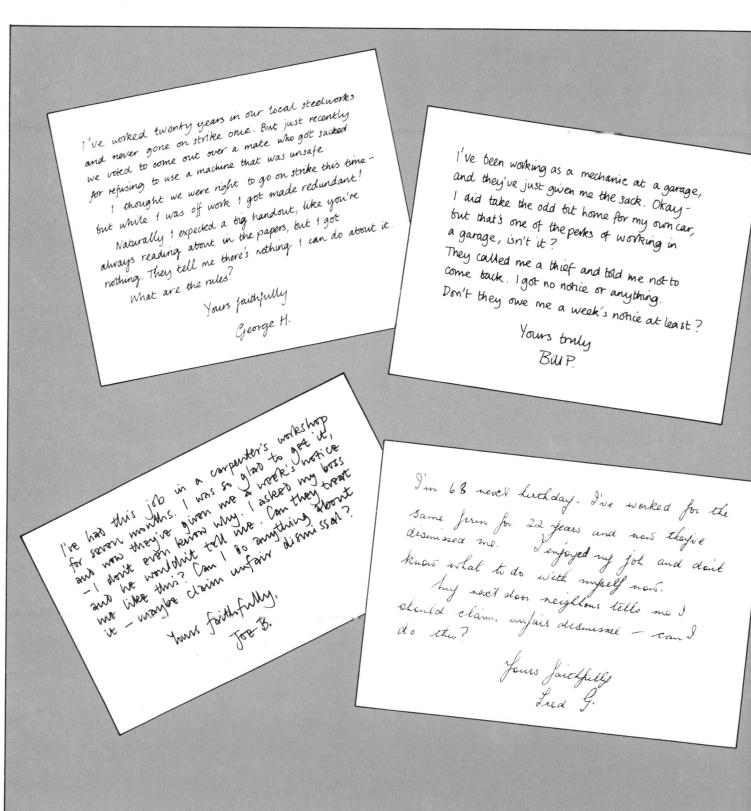

I've worked twenty years in our local steelworks and never gone on strike once. But just recently we voted to come out over a mate who got sacked for refusing to use a machine that was unsafe.

I thought we were right to go on strike this time – but while I was off work I got made redundant!

Naturally I expected a big handout, like you're always reading about in the papers, but I got nothing. They tell me there's nothing I can do about it.

What are the rules?

Yours faithfully
George H.

I've been working as a mechanic at a garage, and they've just given me the sack. Okay – I did take the odd bit home for my own car, but that's one of the perks of working in a garage, isn't it?

They called me a thief and told me not to come back. I got no notice or anything.

Don't they owe me a week's notice at least?

Yours truly
Bill P.

I've had this job in a carpenter's workshop for seven months. I was so glad to get it, and now they've given me a week's notice – I don't even know why. I asked my boss and he wouldn't tell me. Can they treat me like this? Can I do anything about it – maybe claim unfair dismissal?

Yours faithfully,
Joe B.

I'm 68 next birthday. I've worked for the same firm for 22 years and now they've dismissed me. I enjoyed my job and don't know what to do with myself now.

My next door neighbour tells me I should claim unfair dismissal – can I do this?

Yours faithfully
Fred G.

My job was driving a minibus for a hotel, taking passengers to and from the airport. One of the advantages of this job was being allowed the use of the minibus after work. But a couple of weeks ago, on my way home, I called in at the pub for a few drinks with some friends. When I was driving home afterwards I got stopped by the police and breathalysed, and I'm going to be charged with driving when under the influence of drink. Now I've been dismissed from my job. Can they do this to me?

Sincerely
Lesley J.

I have worked as a fashion model in a department store for two years. I recently became pregnant, and told my boss when I was three months pregnant. Two weeks later I got a letter of dismissal.
What can I do? I don't think this was fair - can I go to a tribunal and claim unfair dismissal?

Yours,
Susan M.

I have worked in the same shop full-time for five years. I just couldn't believe it when they made Jane the supervisor instead of me. One morning last week we had an argument in front of a customer. Mr Brown (the manager) warned me that I'd better watch my step and just do what Jane told me to do, but when she wanted me to work through the lunch hour this week I told her where to go. Without any more than that, the manager came down and gave me 2 weeks wages instead of notice. It left me in a mess, as you can believe.

I asked the manager his reason and he said insubordination; but I want to go to an industrial tribunal because the way they gave me notice was unfair and also the amount of notice was wrong.
What is your advice?

Yours
Sarah T.

What would you do?

All of these queries come from people who have had problems at work.

On the next page we have detailed some of the laws concerning employment, grouped under a number of headings.

For each of the letters on this page, see if you can find the relevant section of the employment laws. You should be able to decide what went wrong.

Discuss the details with your group and try to write a reply to each letter, giving advice to Sarah, George, Joe and the others.

- Paid employment is illegal for anyone under thirteen, except in certain family jobs, or on the stage.
- It is generally illegal for children under sixteen to work more than two hours on school days or on Sunday.
- Most authorities do not allow children to work before 7am or after 7pm.
- For a child of school age to work, both the parents and the local authority (usually represented by the head teacher) must be in agreement.

Full time/part time

- If you work for sixteen hours or more a week, you're a full-time worker. Even if you work fewer hours than that, but have been with the same firm for five years or more, you're classed as full-time too.
- If you have a contract to work for sixteen hours a week, but in practice only work eight hours, provided you've been with the firm for six months or more, you're also classed as full-time.

Whether you work full-time or part-time you have certain general rights at work:
- you are protected against victimisation and unfair dismissal if you join a trade union
- You are protected against racial discrimination or discrimination on the grounds of sex or marriage
- you are entitled to equal pay for equivalent work

But you can only expect the following rights if you work full-time:
- written terms of employment
- written reasons for dismissal
- minimum periods of dismissal notice
- redundancy payments
- time off to look for work
- maternity pay and the right to have a job back after having a child
- time off for union duties and protection against unfair dismissal

Maternity

If you're a pregnant woman, you qualify for certain rights if:
- you work full-time
- you have been working for the same employer for at least two years by the eleventh week of your pregnancy
- you don't stop working until the beginning of the eleventh week before the week in which the baby is due

You must also:
- notify your employer at least three weeks before you stop work
- if the employer asks, produce a certificate signed by your doctor or midwife giving the estimated date of the baby's birth

You then have the right to:
- claim unfair dismissal if you are dismissed from your job because you are pregnant
- claim six weeks' maternity pay
- return to the same job up to 29 weeks after the birth, if you have written to your employer:
a) three weeks before you stop work
b) three weeks before you start work again
c) and if, within seven weeks of the baby's birth the employer writes asking you to confirm your return to work, you must reply in writing within two weeks

You also have the right to:
- paid time off to visit clinics
- a maternity grant, whether National Insurance contributions have been paid or not. You must apply for this grant between nine weeks before the baby is due and up to three months after it is born. You can also claim maternity allowance for a number of weeks before and after the birth

Health and Safety

Employers must provide:
- a safe place of work
- a safe system of work
- adequate plant and equipment
- competent staff

If you have an accident at work, however small, report it to whoever keeps the accident book or to the personnel officer. This will protect you if later you find you were injured more seriously than you thought at first.

If you are injured at work or become ill as a result of inadequate safety precautions, you can sue your employer for damages. You need legal help with this.

All workplaces are covered by the Health and Safety at Work Act (1974) which says:
- employers must do what is reasonably possible to look after their employees' health and safety
- an employer of five or more people must put in writing the general policy on health and safety of his or her employees at work. This must be brought to their attention and amended when required

The Health and Safety Executive makes sure the law is carried out. They employ inspectors who have the power to:
- enter and inspect workplaces
- inspect documents, take samples, photograph machinery or equipment
- serve prohibition notices to stop the use of a machine or process where they think there is a serious risk of injury
- serve 'improvement' notices to require a machine or process to be improved in a way which they set out within a set time limit
- prosecute any employer who breaks the health and safety law

Safety representatives

A recognised trade union has the right to appoint a safety representative at the workplace. This person:
- can get information from management about any hazards to workers, such as chemicals used in a factory
- must be consulted by management on any health and safety measures
- has the right to inspect the workplace at least once every three months
- has the right to paid time off to carry out these duties and to attend training courses

rights at work

Dismissal

You have some legal protection against unfair dismissal if:
● you are a full-time worker
● you have been employed by a firm for at least twelve months
● you're under retirement age (60 for a woman and 65 for a man)

Notice

Usually you are entitled to be given notice of your dismissal. The minimum period of notice is:
● one week if you have worked for at least four weeks but less than two years
● one week plus an additional week for each year's continuous service up to a maximum of twelve weeks. However, an employer can ask you to leave immediately and pay you wages instead of asking you to work your notice

You are not entitled to any notice at all if you are dismissed for 'gross misconduct' — for instance, theft.

Before a dismissal

You should be given:
● a warning of any conduct which could lead to your dismissal
● a written warning before dismissal
● a chance to state your case

Reasons for dismissal

If you have worked for a firm for at least six months, you have a right to be given written reasons for your dismissal. You should ask for these as soon as you are sacked. Your employer should give you these within fourteen days. If he or she doesn't, you should complain to an industrial tribunal.

If a firm employs fewer than twenty employees, you're not protected against unfair dismissal until you have worked there for two years. If you want to complain of unfair dismissal to an industrial tribunal, you should seek advice from your trade union, a law centre, or a Citizens' Advice Bureau. You must make your complaint to the tribunal within three months of the end of your notice.

In order to prove a dismissal was fair the employer must show that the reasons for

dismissal were due to one or more of the following:
● your conduct
● your qualifications or capability to do the job
● redundancy (see later)
● your inability to continue employment without you or your employer breaking the law — for example, if your job involved driving and you had lost your licence
● some other substantial reason justifying dismissal

Pregnant women may only be dismissed because of their pregnancy if:
● it makes them incapable of doing the job — for example, heavy lifting
● it's unlawful for them to go on being employed — for example, because of radioactivity in the workplace

If a tribunal decides that a dismissal was unfair they can order:
● reinstatement (which means you go back to the same job with the same pay and conditions)
● re-engagement (which means you are offered another job)
(Both of these orders are rare, however. In 1978, only 3 per cent of people who won their cases got such orders.)
● compensation: this is worked out on a scale, but most compensation awards are low. In 1978, the average was £375

Redundancy

You can be made redundant if:
● your employer stops carrying on business in a certain place
● your work is no longer needed because the requirements of the business have changed

A firm which is planning to make people redundant must consult any recognised trade union within the workplace as early as possible, and must let the Department of Employment know. The firm must also give its employees notice that they are going to be made redundant, along with letters showing how the redundancy payments were worked out.

You can claim redundancy payment if:
● you work full-time
● you have been with the same employer for at least two years since your eighteenth birthday
● you are under retirement age

Certain people, such as National Health workers, cannot claim redundancy payments

You lose your right to redundancy payments if:
● you were on strike when the redundancy notice was sent out
● you accept a different job with the same firm
● you unreasonably refuse suitable alternative employment

If you have been with the firm for at least two years and are going to be made redundant, you must be given a reasonable amount of paid time off to look for a new job or to go on a training course for new work.

Most people at work today have many more rights and protections than they did a century ago, although part-time workers still have fewer advantages than full-time workers. Furthermore, the rights and protections we have are stated in not just one law, but a whole series of laws, and these are so complicated that it is difficult for most people to understand what they mean.

Most people need help on something to do with the law at some point in their lives. For example, they might want to know exactly what their rights are; or what action they can take if they feel they are being treated unfairly by someone else, or by an employer.

There are a number of people and agencies who can give help and advice:

friends
they might be able to advise about where to go for help; this advice costs you nothing

a union representative
if you belong to a union; this advice costs you nothing

a Citizens' Advice Bureau
this advice costs you nothing

a legal aid centre
you may pay nothing, or as much as you can afford

a solicitor
this could cost you money, but you may be able to get legal aid

Equal Opportunities Commission
Overseas House
Quay Street
Manchester M3 3HN
Tel . 061-833 9244
see Glossary. This advice will cost you nothing

Commission for Racial Equality
Elliot House
10/12 Allington Street
London SW1E 5EH
Tel. 01-828 7022
see Glossary. There may be a local office in your area. This advice will cost you nothing

National Council for Civil Liberties
21 Tabard Street
London SE1 4LA
Tel. 01-403 3888
see Glossary. This advice will cost you nothing

national and local radio 'phone-ins'
these occur on a wide range of topics and often offer advice. It costs you nothing but the phone call

letters to newspapers
these can result in advice, information and even support being given. It costs you nothing but the paper and a stamp

List all the laws you can think of which affect your rights at work (you may want to look back to some earlier chapters). Do you think we have too many laws?

Rights

in Conflict

How far can the law go?

Earlier chapters of this book have discussed the reasons why it is necessary to have laws to protect people's freedoms, and how changes in the law can make life better. There has also been discussion of the ways in which laws are made and operated, and by whom.

A good law is one which improves things for the people it is intended to help, and does not leave anyone else worse off. It must be clearly written so that there are no loopholes which enable people to get round it. A lot depends upon the people who operate the law, of course. If the police do not use the law as intended, or if courts make decisions contrary to the original intention of the law, a good law can turn into one which is ineffective or even bad.

Some of the laws discussed in earlier chapters have had disappointing results. For example, The Equal Pay Act 1970 has not made much difference to how much many women earn because employers have been able to find ways to avoid paying women the same as men doing equivalent work (see p. 23). The Sex Discrimination Act 1975 contains so many exclusions (see p. 71) that it has not made much difference to large numbers of women. More people than might have been expected have lost cases brought under The Race Relations Act 1976 (see p. 78).

The problem is that even the best law cannot stop people wanting to discriminate against certain groups. However, a law **can** help people to begin to think differently because it makes them behave differently. For example, women could not become lawyers until 1919 and many people thought that they could not be capable members of the legal profession. Nowadays, more women are becoming lawyers and, even though they are still in a minority (see p. 74), no-one is surprised to see them doing such work. People's **attitudes** have been changed by the law.

Laws do not always give people rights. There have been laws which have taken away rights from large groups of people. For example, a law first prevented women from voting in 1869 (all women finally got the vote in 1928); Roman Catholic men were prevented from becoming MPs in 1678 (they regained the right in 1829). Various immigration laws have affected the right of ethnic minorities to settle in this country.

The law can create as well as solve problems, especially if, in giving rights to one group of people, it takes away rights from another group. An important question to ask about any law is: who benefits most, and who does not benefit, or is worse off, as a result?

How far should the law go?

Another important question which governments sometimes have to consider is whether there can ever be good reason to take away the rights people normally have under the law. For example, as long as we have money to travel, we can usually move about Britain freely. However, in certain situations we might lose that right. If we had a national emergency, such as a war, our free movement around the country might be limited — either to protect us from possible injury, or for reasons of national security.

Sometimes a government's action affecting people's rights leads to controversy or conflict. An example of this is the debate about whether people should be required by law to wear seat-belts in cars. Some people argue that we should keep the right to choose whether or not to wear a seat-belt, and that there have been cases in which people have been trapped in cars when the release mechanism has failed. They are concerned about the increasing number of laws which restrict people's right to make choices. Supporters of the law, however, argue that the wearing of a seat-belt helps to prevent serious injury in the event of an accident, and will not only protect people but also save the health service money.

"If only I'd worn my seat belt."

Department of Transport

Report /Christopher Davies

In Britain, an important right which most people think they have is freedom of speech. Most of us assume that we can say what we like, where we like and when we like. In fact, there are several laws which limit our freedom to express ideas and opinions. It is against The Race Relations Act 1976 to say anything that could be interpreted as incitement to racial hatred. It is against The Official Secrets Acts of 1911, 1920 and 1939 (which are all still in operation) for government employees to disclose certain information, and anyone doing so could be charged with a criminal offence. It is against the law to slander someone (say things about them which are malicious or untrue), to blaspheme, or to speak in such a way that a breach of the peace occurs. It is therefore possible to break several laws at the same time.

The outcome of a charge under any of these laws will depend on how a judge or jury interprets the law. For example, questions have to be raised about exactly what was said, where it was said, to whom, and what effect the speaker's words had on the people around. Did they ignore the speaker, answer back, or become angry or violent? Did a breach of the peace take place, or was it merely a case of obstruction? (That's against the law too.)

One of the problems about many of the rights we have is that other people have them too. Pedestrians have a right to use the road, but so do people driving cars. Having rights means having responsibilities. Just as we want to use our rights, so we have a responsibility to let other people use theirs.

Terry Williams

Sometimes, if we use one kind of right, we take away a different kind of right belonging to someone else. For example, you have a right to express a point of view, but if you shout it out in the street so that other people cannot avoid hearing it, you're taking away their right to choose not to listen or their right not to be disturbed.

Or, if you go to hear someone giving a talk and then heckle them so that they cannot be heard, you could be taking away their right to give an opinion. On the other hand, if they were, for example, expressing racist views, you could argue that you have a responsibility to stop them being heard because they do **not** have a right to incite racial hatred.

The fact that rights can conflict is what makes the business of government so difficult. The government has to decide not only which rights are important, but whether everyone should have the same rights. Having rights means having power, and the government depends on protecting its own powers in order to govern. The problem is that people do not always agree on the best ways to govern. Conflicts can arise which are extremely difficult to resolve. Even making a law cannot settle such conflicts. Indeed it can, in some people's view, make things worse. We are going to look at one law which some people feel has made things worse in one part of the United Kingdom. Other people feel that it has stopped things becoming even worse than they were before. It is a subject which people argue about.

1 Can you think of any rights that people shouldn't have? Give your reasons.

2 Can you think of a right you don't have, that you would like to have?

3 When should demonstrations be banned, if ever?

4 Divide into groups and decide whether people should be compelled to wear seat-belts. What exceptions would you make to this requirement? You might like to report your conclusions to the other groups, and compare the results.

Rights in conflict

Ireland is a divided country. Since 1918 Northern Ireland has been part of the United Kingdom and Southern Ireland (Eire) has been a republic with its own government.

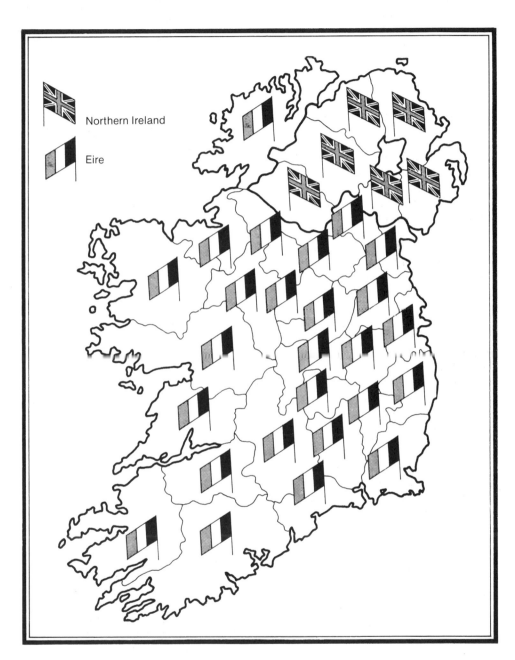

Within Northern Ireland two religious groups are in conflict: Protestants (about a million), and Roman Catholics (about 50 000). Whereas Protestants generally support the link with Britain, many Catholics want Northern Ireland to be re-united with the Catholic Republic of Eire. The history of Northern Ireland is very long and complicated, and people argue about whether the conflict is basically religious or political.

It is not possible to give a brief explanation of the conflict in Northern Ireland. It is possible, however, to look at one law resulting from this conflict which has affected the rights and responsibilities of large numbers of people. This law is The Prevention of Terrorism (Temporary Provisions) Act.

The Prevention of Terrorism Act is the latest in a series of laws passed by the British government in response to acts of terrorism. Due to increasingly violent conflict between Protestant and Catholic groups, British troops were moved to Northern Ireland in 1969. It was hoped that their presence would help to restore peace. However, the conflict has increased and there have been over 10 000 bomb incidents; nearly 2 200 people have been killed;

and more than 22 000 injured. Acts of terrorism have taken place in Britain as well as in Northern Ireland. Following two bomb explosions in Birmingham pubs which killed 21 people, The Prevention of Terrorism Act 1974 was rushed through the Houses of Parliament with almost no opposition. The Act was extended in 1976 and although it has to be renewed every twelve months, renewals have been secured by a large majority ever since.

Acts of terrorism infringe people's basic rights to life, liberty and property. If we each have the right to life, we also each have the responsibility not to endanger other people's lives by violent means. We already have many other laws designed to protect people from violence, but these are not always effective. The Prevention of Terrorism Act 1976 gave the police far greater powers than ever before to combat terrorism.

The Prevention of

P. Jones-Griffiths/Magnum

How the Act has worked

Over 5 000 people have been arrested and detained since 1974. Only 1.6 per cent have been charged with a criminal offence under this Act. A further 7 per cent have been prevented from living in Great Britain by being subjected to an exclusion order.

The Act applies throughout the United Kingdom. The police have the power to:

• arrest and question suspects and detain them for up to seven days
• arrest suspects without a warrant on suspicion of offences connected with terrorism
• photograph and fingerprint suspects without their consent, and use 'reasonable force' if a suspect refuses to co-operate

The Secretary of State has the power to:

• ban terrorist organisations
• make an exclusion order removing someone from Great Britain or Northern Ireland. The person excluded is not charged with a criminal offence and has no right to a court hearing or appeal

In theory, the Act does not oblige people to answer questions, but makes it a criminal offence not to pass information to the police which the person knows or believes might be of assistance to them in preventing an act of terrorism, or in catching, prosecuting, or obtaining a conviction, against someone involved in terrorism.

Terrorism Act

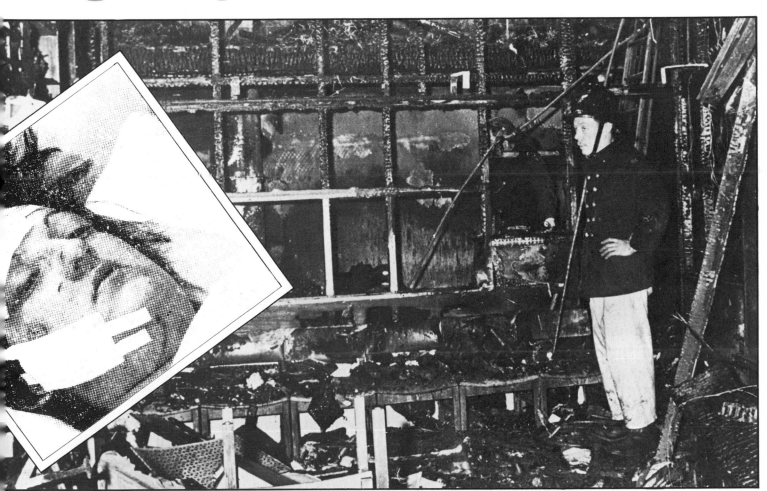

Persons detained during 1980 under The Prevention of Terrorism (Temporary Provisions) Acts 1974 and 1976

Total detained	Number held for more than 48 hrs	Excluded	Charged under Act	Charged under other Acts	Not charged or excluded
537	86	45	11	30	451

While some people would argue that any action that might prevent innocent people being maimed or killed is justified, others say that the action taken by the police under this Act has infringed the rights of many people, taking their liberty away from them and causing inconvenience and distress both to them and their families. The following three examples show what can, and does, happen.

In March 1976 three children were held and interrogated for nearly two days. Their father had committed suicide on the morning of their arrest. Their mother was also arrested and questioned, but was later acquitted on a charge concerning terrorist activity.

In November 1977 a twelve year old girl was taken into police custody for several hours while her parents were detained and relatives were found to look after her. She complained that she was fingerprinted, asked about her parents, and asked whether she could recognise a man whose photograph was shown to her.

In February 1978 a man was arrested under The Prevention of Terrorism Act and detained for questioning. Later he was transferred to Brixton prison, served with an exclusion order, and flown to Belfast. The man had come to live in Britain five years earlier and had married an English woman.

Like other excluded people, he was not arrested when he arrived at his destination, and he returned to the Catholic estate in Belfast where he had grown up. His English wife, who is not a Catholic, and their two daughters decided they had no choice but to follow him.

The Kent solicitor who acted for the man said:
'The Act ... works extremely harshly and no doubt unfairly in such cases where there must be a real doubt as to whether or not he was really involved in any terrorist activities in Northern Ireland or in England which would have justified his exclusion from England ... His wife is English and the two children were born in England (and) the exclusion order virtually forced her and the children to leave their country of origin.'

The solicitor also pointed out that, since the suspect faced with an exclusion order is never charged with a criminal offence, no legal aid is available. The person has to pay for advice or depend on the willingness of a solicitor to take on the case without payment.

A further argument against the Act is that the minority of people charged with criminal offences could have been arrested and charged under normal police powers. Therefore the Act is thought by many not to be necessary and, because it takes away rights from so many people, should be repealed.

1 Look back at pages 30-35, and compare the powers of the police listed there with the powers they have under The Prevention of Terrorism Act.
2 Look again at the powers the police have under The Prevention of Terrorism Act. What are the arguments for and against them retaining these powers?
3 Throughout history there have been examples of people using violence to get what they want. Look at the following statements and discuss whether or not you agree with each one, giving your reasons for doing so.
• Violent acts are never justified in any circumstances
• Violent acts are sometimes justified as long as no-one gets hurt
• No-one ever has the right to damage public or private property
• Even if you do not intend any people to get hurt, violence sometimes results in them getting injured or killed; therefore it is a risk that should never be taken
• If you really believe in something, you can justify any kind of behaviour to achieve it
• Peaceful demonstrations achieve more than violent demonstrations
• It can be legitimate to damage public property but it can never be legitimate to damage private property

Points for teachers

The following brief notes are designed to provide teachers with additional information relating to some of the questions raised in this book, and with ideas for helping students to engage in discussion of important issues.

A range of *questions* is provided on each topic so that students can exercise choices and can extend their knowledge and understanding of aspects in which they feel a particular interest. Many of the questions, particularly those of an open-ended nature, lend themselves both to group debate and to written activities: their purpose is to encourage consideration and comparison of alternative viewpoints. Some questions demand factual answers: where these cannot be elicited from the text, details are given below.

What would you do? boxes are generally group activities. Classes used to working in small groups will probably have no difficulty in organising themselves. Those to whom this is unfamiliar may welcome some help from the teacher — for example, in sharing out tasks and presenting their conclusions. In mixed ability classes, it might be profitable to ensure that each group includes a mixed range of abilities. In mixed sex classes, it is also important that groups are mixed to avoid a stereotyped polarisation of views.

Chapter One

Why Laws?

Page 11, question 3

This might provide a useful homework assignment by encouraging each student to summarise the results of the group activities.

Page 21, *What would you do?*

1 The purpose of this exercise is to encourage students to consider questions from a variety of different viewpoints, and to weigh up the answers that they feel might be seen as most important. For example, it could be argued that both employees are involved in a similar activity: preparing food. The following points would need to be considered:

• their job titles (Is Mr Dancy employed as a chef? a cook? a supervisor?)
• their job descriptions
• how their time is spent
• the number of people they cater for
• what differences there might be between cooking lunch for a group of directors and for a large body of employees (for example, the directors might expect more complicated dishes, the employees more choice of dishes)

• what actual hours are worked
• what holidays the two people are entitled to
• whether they receive any fringe benefits (for example, free meals), and if so, what
• what assistance they receive
• whether the shopping is done for them
• whether they have to make orders involving paperwork, etc.

Some students might like to treat this case as if they were members of an industrial tribunal, dividing into groups to work out arguments in support of or against the claims of Ms Graham. These could then be presented and the groups could take a vote. (This exercise is based on a real case where the woman succeeded in her claim for equal pay.)

2 The purpose of this activity is to encourage students to explore the complexities involved in trying to frame laws. If a law is not to create more problems than it solves, it must be clearly worded, precise and unambiguous. It must clearly state the persons to whom it applies, and the persons to whom it does not apply or who are exempted from some or all of its terms. It may be necessary to include scope for action in the event of its being ignored or disobeyed. The creation of an agency to encourage its implementation might be necessary, for example the Equal Opportunities Commission, or sanctions for those who disobey, for example fines for not wearing a seat-belt. Discussion of the laws the students frame could be extended to listing the questions one might ask about any law and then looking in detail at, for example, The Equal Pay Act, to see how far it meets the criteria which have been decided upon.

Some students might find it difficult to decide upon a law to frame. If so, teachers might suggest an example such as a law raising the cost of dog licences — currently 37½p (unchanged since 1878). They may need to be reminded of possible valid exemptions, for example guide dogs for the blind. Another suggestion for a new law might be one to prevent people smoking on any part of public transport.

Page 23, question 1

Students may offer some sex-stereotyped answers to this question — for example, that women don't need to earn as much as men. They might be surprised to learn that 1/5 of family breadwinners in Britain are women, and that over 1 000 000 families are single-parent families. Reasons which have been recorded by industrial tribunals for not giving equal pay to people doing the same jobs include: employees on protected salaries; long service awards; and merit awards for training.

Chapter Two

Policing

Page 7, question 5

Students are likely to produce a fairly comprehensive list. If not, discussing the variety of situations and people a police officer might meet may stimulate their thinking. For example, knowledge of behaviour associated with mental illness would be an asset; and in a multi-racial society, the ability to speak one or more foreign languages would help.

Page 7, question 6

This question is also likely to produce a range of answers — for example, the general public's attitude to the police frequently means that officers are not comfortably accepted in social situations; the training that police officers receive results in the development of habits of observation which they may find difficult not to practise when off-duty. It is hoped that students will appreciate the social isolation and ever-present obligations that many police feel.

Pages 30 and 31, Police powers

The suggestions under *Some police want greater powers* come from the evidence given by Sir David McNee (Commissioner of the Metropolitan Police) to the Royal Commision on Criminal Procedure, 1979.

The examples are hypothetical situations for discussion purposes.

Search on arrest
The police may search a person and the premises on which he or she is arrested at the time of the arrest. In this example, when the police searched the other premises, they were only acting lawfully if the owners of the property had been asked for and had given their consent.

Search with a warrant
The police should have reasonable suspicion of wrong-doing in order to apply for a warrant. In practice, a written statement about the reasonable suspicion is usually accepted by a magistrate.

Search without a warrant or arrest
All the requests are reasonable and should be satisfied: the police may not wish to give their names but are obliged to give their numbers.

Arrest without a warrant
The member of the right wing group could have been arrested in these circumstances for behaviour likely to cause a breach of the peace. A subsequent charge of incitement to racial hatred could be brought with the permission of the Director of Public Prosecutions.

Detention
The police officer could not arrest Alan for playing in a children's playground. If a person has not been arrested, he or she cannot be forced to go to a police station.

Record keeping
The police cannot force Jane to have her photograph taken. However, they can apply for a magistrate's order to take her fingerprints. If this is given (it is not automatic), then Jane would have the right to see her fingerprint record destroyed if she were subsequently acquitted.

Page 32, *What would you do?*

This activity page has been inserted to help students consolidate their basic understanding of the police officer's role, and the powers the police have, before they consider more detailed information on each of these powers.

Page 33, Search

There are already many circumstances in which a search warrant may be obtained, and many organisations recommend a tightening up of the procedure for search warrants. Their recommendations include the following:
• the police should be made to inform the magistrate of the name of any informant on whose testimony they are acting
• a record should be made whenever a warrant is granted, and the results noted
• each search warrant should allow one search only, and last for a set period of, for example, two weeks
• a warrant should always allow an arrested person, or his or her solicitor, to be present at the search of that person's premises
• material not used in evidence should be returned within three months of seizure

Pages 34 and 35, Arrest

It should be pointed out to students that not all court cases are started by arrest. Most civil cases and a large number of criminal cases are started by a summons. This is an order requiring a person's attendance to answer certain charges. If the order is ignored, the person is likely to be arrested.

Question 3b

Tape recording would provide accurate records of conversations between the police and suspects. This would prevent malicious allegations by suspects about events in the police station. The police argue:
• if the suspects knew that their conversation was being recorded, they might be inhibited. They might not want to talk about accomplices, for example, as they could not later deny being the source
• tape recorders might break down
• suspects might talk quietly and might nod or shake their heads
• two people being interviewed at the same time might be indistinguishable on tape

A written record of what a suspect said in a police station is often presented in court as important evidence by the prosecution. They argue that this is nearer the truth than later evidence, as the suspect has not had the opportunity to invent a careful story. Therefore it is crucial to have an accurate record of what is said at the police station. The police invest many thousands of pounds in researching and manufacturing equipment for watching people and for storing information. The expense of financing a tape recording system might well be offset by the saving of court time on challenges to the accuracy of police records.

Question 4

The police national computer contains a national fingerprint index. If a person has been arrested and has given fingerprints without a court order being obtained, the police are not obliged to destroy them even if the person is not charged or is subsequently acquitted.
Many people refuse to give their fingerprints to the police voluntarily, either because they want to be difficult or because they have genuine fears that the police may not destroy the records subsequently.

Chapter Three

Courts, Crime and Punishment

The story of Luke Dougherty is one of the cases dealt with in great detail in the *Report to the Secretary of State for the Home Department of the Departmental Committee on Evidence of Identification in Criminal Cases* (HMSO 1976), commonly known as the Devlin Report. It has been chosen as an example because an unlikely combination of circumstances led to a miscarriage of justice and therefore the case went through all the stages from the Magistrates' Court to the Court of Appeal. Many of the questions during the unfolding of the story are designed to be answered both from the facts given in the text and also from the information given on pp. 52-66 at the end of the chapter. This is to encourage the exercise of reference skills and a flexible use of the book. The experience of working through the case stage by stage will introduce pupils to the complexities of a system of criminal justice which depends upon the prosecution proving guilt, and which operates by a well-established set of procedures. The case illustrates that if, at any one stage, these procedures are inadequately or improperly carried out, a miscarriage of justice can result. It also illustrates that it is sometimes possible for a legal decision to be overturned. Additionally, in this case, public campaigning initiated by one person, who knew beyond doubt that Luke Dougherty was innocent of the charge, resulted in a reversal of the court's decision. This demonstrates that the ordinary citizen can play an important role in the machinery of justice.

Theft, question 1

To be accused of shoplifting, a person must have left the premises with the goods. If stopped while still on the premises, the person could claim that he or she had every intention of paying for the goods.

Theft, question 2

PC Anderson should have taken descriptions

of all three witnesses. He failed to make a full report of the incident. A team is easier to discover than a single operator, and an elderly woman with a limp more easily identified than a man without distinguishing marks. An enquiry about the woman might have produced the name of a suspect, and she would have had no association with Luke Dougherty. PC Anderson also failed to obtain or record a description of the thief from Miss Mallin.

Identification, page 45

Students may be interested to know what happens at an identification parade.

A suspect is placed in a line with a number of other people of similar age, height and general appearance and of the same sex. The subject is allowed to change that position after each witness has left. The suspect may object to any of the members of the parade or to the arrangements. No intimation as to the suspect's identify should be given to the witness.

Magistrates' Court, question 1

The system of lay magistrates has a number of advantages which might appeal to an accused person. Magistrates' Courts are less formal than higher courts and JPs, unlike judges, are often in touch with, and represent, trade unions and business, so their experience is nearer to that of the ordinary person. JPs are appointed in recognition of their public service; although not legally qualified, they receive advice from qualified Clerks of the Court, and there is always more than one JP hearing a case. The underlying principle is that citizens should participate in our system of justice.

On the other hand, an accused person may be deterred from electing for trial in a Magistrates' Court by the possibility that, being drawn from the locality, magistrates may not be able to view either the accused or the circumstances leading to the trial without prejudice. The social composition of JPs is restricted — they tend to be middle-aged (or older) and middle class, and some people feel that they deal more harshly with social types they dislike, so that there are wide variations in the sentences given to different people for the same offence. They frequently fail to justify or give reasons for their verdicts and are sometimes accused of being uncritical of police evidence. It has been known for magistrates to bind over people even when they have been found innocent of any charges or were merely trial witnesses.

A further criticism of lay magistrates is that the appointing committees are dominated by party politicians, who nominate their own members for the position. The composition of appointment committees is kept secret, as is the appointment process, so the possibility of change seems remote.

Magistrates' Court, question 2

It is suggested that students may like to refer ahead to the magistrate's account of her work, and the way Magistrates' Courts operate, in order to help them understand why Luke Dougherty opted for trial by jury. Since magistrates are recruited from local people, it is likely that Luke Dougherty would have been recognised and his criminal record recalled by a local magistrate: he therefore felt that he would have a fairer trial by jury.

Defence, question 1

The Devlin Report indicates that neither the prosecution nor the defence treated Luke Dougherty's alibi very seriously: the prosecution possibly because they thought it an unlikely story; the defence because they were convinced of its truth. The Report also held that the solicitor's work in assisting Luke Dougherty to establish an alibi was 'quite inadequate'. 'He left it to Mr Dougherty to select the witnesses, though ... he vetoed some names. He did not verify that the witnesses had no previous convictions ... The brief delivered to his counsel shows that only the most perfunctory investigation was made.' As a result, the times and departure of the coach were incorrectly given by the defence, and the calling of only two witnesses out of the 30 or 40 available meant that the picture of Luke Dougherty's movements on the day in question was far from complete. Therefore his alibi was unconvincing. In addition, the police report on the interviewing of alibi witnesses did not prompt the prosecution to reconsider the merits of their case. The Devlin Report concluded that all the preliminary stages of the investigation were inadequately conducted. Had the alibi been thoroughly investigated, the case might never have been brought.

Crown Court, question 3

Mr Fenwick thought that the prosecution's case was weak on three points:
• an identification parade had not been held despite Luke Dougherty's expressed willingness to attend
• both Miss Mallin and Mr Butterfield had been shown police photographs of Luke Dougherty, thus raising the possibility that they had identified him as the thief from their memories of the photographs rather than of the incident which led to the trial; additionally, the existence of the photographs could have led them to suspect that he had a criminal record which, although irrelevant to the case in hand, might have predisposed them to believe in his guilt on this particular charge
• only one of the two witnesses had given a description of the thief and the colour of his hair — which was quite different from Luke Dougherty's

It seemed unlikely that a conviction could be secured in these circumstances. Although Mr Fenwick's advice was reasonable in the light of the points made above, had the case been adjourned, more witnesses to support Luke Dougherty's contention that he had not committed the offence could have been called.

Verdict, page 49

In his summing up of the case (which the Devlin Report described as 'beyond criticism') the judge advised the jury to treat the evidence of identification with particular caution as 'identification mistakes are very easy to make and you should approach the evidence of identification with extreme scepticism, so that in the end you look for something that convinces you that the identification is right.' He later commented that 'Dock identifications are extremely dangerous.'

It is significant that the jury was out for nearly two hours before reaching a unanimous verdict — an indication that some, at least, had doubted the prosecution's case.

Campaign and Appeal, question 1

Fresh evidence can be brought to an Appeal Court only by the permission of the judge who has considered the application for leave to appeal. This permission is usually only given if evidence has come to light that was not available at the time of the original hearing. In this case, the evidence had been available — there were 30 to 40 witnesses who could have confirmed Luke Dougherty's alibi — but they were not called. The judge who heard the application decided therefore that the grounds for hearing fresh evidence were not adequate. This meant that Luke Dougherty's case was weakened; the information which could convince the Appeal Court of his innocence could not be cited.

Campaign and Appeal, question 2

Luke Dougherty was sentenced on 22 February 1973; his application for leave to appeal was first heard on 9 May 1973. On 20 June, Luke Dougherty received a letter in prison from the Registrar of Criminal Appeals asking him, amongst other things, whether he wanted Mr Fenwick to continue to represent him at the hearing. The Registrar also advised him that if he did not, and another barrister had to be found to take on the case, there might be considerable delay before the case was heard. Having already been in prison for four months for an offence he had not committed, it is not surprising that Luke Dougherty preferred to retain Mr Fenwick's services. However, according to the Devlin Report, Mr Fenwick was not optimistic about the outcome of the application for leave to appeal — because he would not be able to bring the fresh evidence which had been collected.

Additionally, Mr Fenwick felt some embarrassment about the fact that he had advised Luke Dougherty against an adjournment during the original trial; had the case been adjourned and more witnesses called, Luke Dougherty might not have been convicted. A new barrister would have been able to use all the available evidence, including that which had emerged since the trial. First, a barrister willing to take the case would have to be found, and second, he or she would need more time to prepare for the hearing than Mr Fenwick, who was already familiar with the case. As a result, Luke Dougherty might have had to remain in prison even longer before his application to appeal was dealt with.

Page 66, Sentencing map

This map shows the percentage of males aged 21 and over who were found guilty of

indictable offences and sentenced to immediate imprisonment in 1973 in England and Wales. The variation in the percentages of adult men sent to prison suggests:
• the same laws may be differently enforced in different parts of the country
• magistrates may be stricter in some parts of the country than in others
• the unlikely possibility that there is a greater proportion of criminals in some parts of the country than in others

Chapter Four

Equal (almost) under the Law

This chapter aims to introduce students to the concept of discrimination, focusing on discrimination on grounds of gender, race and sexuality, and on the legislation which has been introduced to combat it.
The case of Farhath Malik on p. 80 illustrates the procedures involved in taking a case to an industrial tribunal, and how hearings are conducted.

Page 69, question 3

The purpose of this question is to encourage students to look beyond the surface meaning and immediate impact of advertisements to the more indirect and subtle messages they frequently incorporate. For example, men are often shown as taller than women and as directing and instructing women; women are often shown sitting on the floor at men's feet, doing domestic work, or day-dreaming. It is rare for either sex to be shown engaged in non-traditional activities.

Page 69, question 6

Teachers may like to provide statistics on the numbers of girls studying science subjects. The following table gives the numbers of GCE O level entries in 1976.

Subject	Boys	Girls
English Lit	106 000	141 000
English Lang	183 000	203 000
French	66 000	84 000
Maths	116 000	87 000
Chemistry	60 000	30 000
Physics	86 000	25 000
Biology	61 000	86 000

From A. Clwyd, 'Reversing the Pecking Order', *Guardian* 7 July 1977. Quoted in R. Deem, *Women and Schooling*, London, Routledge and Kegan Paul 1978.

Chapter Five

Leaving School

The purpose of this chapter is to introduce students to some of the issues involved in leaving school, and to some of the rights and responsibilities they will assume as young adults. As realistic a picture as possible has been attempted through the fictional account of the fortunes of three young people. It is hoped that students will realise that they need to make informed and sensible choices about their behaviour and any opportunities for employment, and that choices they make at this age will have a strong influence on their future.

Chapter Six

Rights in Conflict

This chapter attempts to draw together some of the main aspects of rights, responsibilities and the law which have been introduced and dwelt upon in earlier chapters. It is hoped that by the time they reach this chapter, students will have developed
• a critical consciousness of the purposes, functions, and limitations of law as a regulatory system in our society
• some awareness of the relationship between people's rights as private individuals and their duties as citizens
• some insights into the problems involved in reconciling different, sometimes conflicting, interests

The main purpose of this final chapter is to assist students to appreciate that, when rights conflict, there are no simple solutions. Actions taken for the good of the community as a whole may result in suffering or hardship for some people. The question is not so much whether a price has to be paid, but who it should be paid by. The last section of the chapter focuses upon The Prevention of Terrorism Act 1976 because it raises fundamental civil liberties issues for citizens of the United Kingdom, of which Northern Ireland is a part. The historical background to the current conflict is extremely complex and no brief summary could accurately reflect the perspectives of the various protagonists and the events of the last few hundred years. For this reason, only the barest information to set the Act in context is recounted. It is hoped that students will
• deplore acts of terrorism as violations of the most basic human rights
• adopt a questioning approach towards laws such as The Prevention of Terrorism Act which, whilst on the one hand are intended to protect human rights, on the other may result in the undermining of those same rights
• appreciate that different groups may have different opinions about an issue, and that dialogue and dissent can result in a clarifying of important ideas

Page 108, question 3

The purpose of this activity is to encourage students to reflect upon the differences between morally legitimate and morally illegitimate forms of protest, and to discuss and justify their own viewpoints. They may need some assistance in clarifying what they understand by phrases such as 'peaceful demonstration', 'public property'.

Teachers may like to recommend some further reading to students who are interested in more background to the topics raised in this book. The National Council for Civil Liberties have published:

First Rights: a guide to legal rights for young people by Maggie Rae, Patricia Hewitt and Barry Hugill, 1979

Know your rights: NCCL factsheets, 1978

Glossary

The following definitions and descriptions relate to the use of terms in a legal context; some of the words included have alternative meanings in everyday use.

accuse
to charge with an act against the law

acquit
to declare an accused person to be innocent of a charge; to release

adjourn
to postpone, or cause an interval in, the hearing of a case

Advisory, Conciliation and Arbitration Service (ACAS)
an independent organisation set up under The Employment Protection Act 1975 to provide help in conciliation, mediation and arbitration to avoid and resolve industrial disputes

alibi
the claim of someone accused of a crime that he or she was elsewhere when the crime was committed

appeal
to apply to a higher court against a lower court's decision

Appeal Court
see Court of Appeal

apprehend
to arrest or seize

approved school
a special school to which young offenders are sent when it is felt that they need to be removed from home, or that they need punishment by withdrawal of their liberty

arbitration
the decision of someone chosen to judge

arrest
to seize and hold legally; a member of the public may make a 'citizen's arrest' in certain circumstances

arrestable offence
a crime for which the police may arrest a suspect without a warrant

arson
the crime of setting fire to property

assessment
the act of fixing an amount, e.g. damages for injuries received

bail
a sum of money, or security, demanded by police or by a court to obtain temporary release of a prisoner who has not yet come to trial

barrister
a lawyer qualified to plead in a law court on behalf of either the prosecution or the defence

bench
the judge, or the magistrates, in court

bill
a draft of a proposed Act of Parliament

binding over
see p. 58

blaspheme
to use language which offends people's religious beliefs

borstal
a place where young boys are detained and receive corrective training

breach of the peace
behaviour which causes public disorder

campaign
an organised attempt to interest the public in something and persuade them to give support

caution
a warning, or to give a warning

census
an official counting of the population

Citizens' Advice Bureau
a centre where people can go for information and advice

civil law
cases relating to disputes between citizens over property and legal relations; not criminal law

civil servants
paid administrative staff of Government departments

clerk of the court
an official in a court of law who keeps records and advises magistrates on points of law

commission
a body of people appointed to investigate an issue

Commission for Racial Equality
a body set up under The Race Relations Act 1976 to work towards the elimination of discrimination, and to promote equality of opportunity and good relations between people of different racial groups

commit
to send for trial, or send to prison

committal proceedings
a preliminary hearing in front of magistrates to ascertain whether there are sufficient grounds to commit an accused person for trial

compensation
a payment, usually in money, to make amends for a crime

confine
to limit a person's actions, usually by imprisonment

constitutional
agreeing with the laws of the state

contract
the agreement of fixed terms usually, but not necessarily, in writing

convict
to find guilty in court

conviction
a record of a verdict of guilty

credit-worthiness
an estimate of a person's suitability to borrow money, based on his or her record of solvency (not owing money) or repayment of previous loans or debts

Crown Court
a major court which deals with indictable criminal offences and with civil matters; cases are heard by judges

counsel
a lawyer qualified to represent a client in court; a barrister

County Court
an area court which deals with disputes relating to contracts, trusts, mortgages and a variety of other matters such as adoption of children

Court of Appeal
the court where a convicted person, or a person who has lost a case, can ask for the conviction to be quashed or a decision to be reversed. Cases are heard by three judges

custody
imprisonment pending trial; given the keeping of (a child)

defence
the argument claiming innocence of, or justifying, an act which has led to someone being charged with an offence

defendant
a person accused of an offence in a court of law

detention
the condition of being restrained or kept under guard

detention centre
a place where young people found guilty of an offence are detained as a punishment and for correction

deterrent
anything that will prevent or discourage a particular kind of behaviour occurring or recurring

detriment
a disadvantage; a damage

discharge
to release or to acquit (see also p. 58)

discriminate
to distinguish between; to treat less favourably

dismissal
the act of dismissing or sending away; removing from employment

dock
the place where the accused person stands in court

edulcorator
a sweetener

elect
to choose by vote

electoral register
a list of people entitled to vote

employment appeal tribunal
a body to which a claimant or an employer who has lost a case at an industrial tribunal can appeal for the decision to be reconsidered

enforce
to compel people to obey a law, usually by the threat of punishment for disobedience

equal opportunity
the same chance to compete in all aspects of life regardless of sex, race, colour, or national origin

Equal Opportunities Commission
a body set up under The Sex Discrimination Act 1975 to fight sex discrimination and to encourage equal opportunities for men and women

equal pay
the same pay for the same work, or work which has been rated as 'broadly similar' by a job evaluation scheme

ethnic
concerning race

European Court of Justice
a court comprising judges selected from all the member states of the EEC (see below) which hears cases brought by those member states, EEC institutions and individuals

European Economic Community
a group of countries/states which have agreed to share the same rights and obligations. Britain joined on 1 January 1973

evaluator
someone who values the worth of something, usually in terms of money. In job evaluation schemes, he or she estimates the value or comparability of jobs

evidence
information given in court to establish a fact

exception
something that is left out, or different from the rest

exclusion order
an order preventing someone from travelling to, or residing in, a particular place (see also p.110)

exempt
to be granted immunity from, to be free of a duty imposed on others

gay
sexually attracted to persons of the same sex as oneself

Green Paper
a discussion document issued by the government as a preliminary to a proposed change in law

guilty
having committed an offence; or having been judged to have committed an offence

heckle
to interrupt a public speaker with questions or statements

heterosexual
sexually attracted to the opposite sex

High Court
a court which deals with civil actions, appeals from lower courts, and various special kinds of law

homosexual
sexually attracted to persons of the same sex as oneself

House of Commons
House of Parliament to which members are elected by the public

House of Lords
House of Parliament in which hereditary and life peers are entitled to sit

identification
establishing the identity of a person

identification parade
a line-up of at least eight people (including a suspect) to be inspected by a witness

illegal
against the law

immigration
the entry into a country as residents of people from another country

incite
to stir up; to urge on

indictable offence
an offence for which a person can be tried by a jury

industrial tribunal
a panel of three people who hear complaints brought under employment laws

interpret
to explain or understand the meaning of

interrogate
to question thoroughly; to cross-examine

job evaluation
a scheme by which it is decided whether two jobs are of the same value and thus merit equal pay

judge
an official (usually trained as a barrister) appointed to try accused persons in court, or to hear civil cases

Judges' Rules
see p. 34

jurisdiction
the extent of a court's power

jury
a body of people (usually twelve) chosen to decide on a verdict after hearing evidence in court

Justice
see p. 55

Justice of the Peace (JP)
see p. 54

juvenile
a person aged under seventeen

Juvenile Court
a special court which is less formal than a Magistrates' Court where young people over ten and under seventeen are tried for offences. The public is not allowed to attend and there are reporting restrictions

law
rules recognised or made by government as binding on people's behaviour

legal aid
the money provided by the state to pay the costs of a legal action

legislation
the making of laws

legitimate
lawful; justifiable

lesbian
a woman homosexual

lobby
to try to influence a Member of Parliament to favour a particular cause

Lord Chancellor
a member of the House of Lords, who is the head of the judicial system in this country

Lord Lieutenant
the ancient title for the nominal head of a country who advises the Lord Chancellor about the appointment of county magistrates. Women can hold this position

magistrate
see p. 54

Magistrates' Court
a local court which deals mainly with criminal offences but also with some civil matters and licensing of premises (see also pp. 54, 64)

management
people responsible for administration

matrimonial orders
court decisions relating to marriage

minority
the smaller number (less than half of the total)

minority group
see p. 67

mitigation
circumstances which may make an offence receive less severe punishment

motion
a proposal put before a meeting

National Council for Civil Liberties
a campaigning organisation which defends human rights in the UK and assists individuals to bring cases claiming their rights

National Insurance
a compulsory payment towards public service deducted from wages and salaries

National Insurance Card
a record of a person's National Insurance number

negotiate
to bargain with

notice of assessment
a statement from the Department of Health and Social Security showing how a person's benefit has been worked out; also from Inland Revenue about how tax payable has been worked out

obstruction
anything that gets in the way of, or hinders progress

offence
the breaking of the law; a wrongdoing; a crime

offensive weapon
an object which could be used to attack someone

Official Secrets Act, The
(in fact, a series of Acts) which prohibit the communication of certain kinds of Government information

ombudsman
an official (can be a woman) who decides on the validity of complaints made against government departments and local authorities

oppression
cruel and harsh treatment; tyranny

Parole Board
a board set up by the Home Office, consisting of four members, who consider applications from prisoners for early release

penal
involving punishment

petition
a written request signed by many people

picket
people stationed to deter would-be workers during a strike

plea
a defendant's answer to a charge in a court of law

Police National Computer
the computer containing police records on individuals

precedent
a happening in the past which may serve as an example in the future

pressure group
a group exerting political influences

Private Member's Bill
a bill put forward by an ordinary Member of Parliament, rather than as an official government measure (see also p. 24)

probation
see p. 58

procedure
the routine to follow

proceedings
a legal action

prosecute
to take legal action against a person

prosecutor
the officer who prosecutes in court

provision
a clause in the law

questionnaire
a series of questions to obtain information on a specific subject

racial discrimination
unfavourable treatment of individuals because of their race or national origin

redundancy
dismissal of workers no longer needed

reform
to improve; to do better

Registrar of Criminal Appeals
an official concerned with the administration of the Court of Appeal (Criminal Division)

rehabilitate
to restore to previous condition; to make fit

reinstate
to re-establish a former condition

remand
to keep in custody while awaiting trial

represent
to argue on another person's behalf

republic
a government without a monarch

right
a just or legal claim of entitlement, e.g. to life, to liberty, to freedom of speech

Secretary of State for Education
a Member of Parliament, who is appointed to the Cabinet by the Prime Minister, with responsibility for the provision of state education

sentence
the punishment given to an offender after a verdict of guilty has been pronounced by the court

settlement
an agreement

sex discrimination
unfavourable treatment of individuals because of their sex (most often applies to women, but can apply to men)

sheriff
the chief officer in a county or distict

shop
the term used for a place of employment (e.g. a factory) where the workers are unionised

shop steward
an official elected by trade union members to represent them in negotiations with the union and with management

slander
a false statement (spoken, not written) meant to damage a person's character

solicitor
a lawyer who gives legal advice and prepares documents for court cases

Special Patrol Group
a group of highly trained police officers, all with firearms experience, who deal with exceptional situations

statement
a formal account of an event

stereotype
a representation based on generalisations about a particular group e.g. women, blacks, students

stipendiary magistrate
a full-time, paid magistrate

sue
to bring legal action in a civil court

suffragette
a woman who campaigned for the right to vote using militant means

summary offence
see p. 54

summing up
going over previous arguments and evidence

summons
a written order to appear in court

supervision order
an order imposed by a court where the guilty person is supervised — e.g. by a probation officer. It can contain restrictions, e.g. on place of residence, travel, who the person can associate with

supplementary benefit
money paid by the State to people who are without employment or are retired, whose other income is below a fixed minimum

surety
a legal safeguard (usually money) offered as security against someone's failure to appear to answer a charge in court; bail

suspect
a person who is thought to be guilty of a crime

tax year
the twelve-month period used for accounting purposes: from 6 April of one year to 5 April of the next

terrorism
the use of terror, or intimidation, to achieve a purpose

testify
to give evidence in court

trade union
an organised association of workers

transit card
a card given by the careers office to an unemployed young person which he or she then has to produce at an unemployment benefit office

tribunals
bodies appointed to arbitrate in disputes between individuals and, e.g., employers, landlords, DHSS

unanimous
agreed to by everybody

unemployment benefit
(the dole) money levied by the State and paid to people who are out of work

usher
a doorkeeper; officer who escorts people to their places

vandalism
the careless or deliberate destruction of property

verdict
judgement or decision of the jury or judge

vet
to examine carefully and critically

victimisation
the act of subjecting someone to ill-treatment, of causing to suffer

voluntary organisation
a group of people working for a cause, sometimes with some government funding, more often raising money themselves

warrant
a writ giving police authority to arrest a person or to carry out an act (e.g. a search)

White Paper
Government proposals for a new law

witness
a person giving sworn evidence in court

Youth Opportunities Programme
a series of short-term training and work experience schemes set up by the government for unemployed young people

Index

Acknowledgments

The publishers acknowledge with thanks the help of the following teachers:

Yvonne Beecham, ILEA advisory teacher: Social Studies
Bob Dade, Broxbourne School, Broxbourne, Herts
Margaret Donnellan, Calder High School, Mytholmroyd, West Yorks
Heather Flint, Hurlingham School, ILEA
Rebecca Foster, Bethnal Green Institute (now Tower Hamlets Institute), ILEA
David Griffiths, Ebbw Vale Comprehensive School, Ebbw Vale, Gwent
Tim Hall, St Paul's Way School, ILEA
David Head, Mary Ward Settlement, ILEA
Audrey Hodge, Hopefield Secondary School, Newtownabbey, Co. Antrim, Northern Ireland
Maggie Howell, Pimlico School, ILEA
Gerrison Lansdown, Loughton College of FE, Loughton, Essex
Bert MacIver, Hackney Downs School, ILEA
Brian Merton, Kingsway-Princeton College, ILEA
Bryan Reece and Rob Webb
Northgate High School, Dereham, Norfolk
David Roche, St Bede's Grammar School, Bradford, West Yorks
Martin Straker-Wells, Pimlico School, ILEA
Jan Thornton, Kingsway-Princeton College, ILEA
Sue Twining, Clapton School, ILEA
Barry Varley-Tipton, Quintin Kynaston School, ILEA

Thanks are also due to the following:

Preet and Harsev Bains
Malcolm Hurwitt
Martin Kettle
Lancashire Constabulary
Inspector C.M. Leithead
Kuttan Menon
Ron Pepper
Belinda Price
the Poyser family
Stephen Sedley
Vishnu Sharma
Peter Thornton
and to the judge, barrister, solicitor and magistrate featured on pages 52 to 54.

Endocil Ltd and Butler Dennis Garland and Partners Ltd would like us to print out that the Endocil advertisement featured on page 68 is no longer in use.

The forms on pages 88 and 89 are reproduced by permission of the Controller of Her Majesty's Stationery Office.